José
MOURINHO

José MOURINHO

» Made in Portugal

Luís Lourenço

José MOURINHO

By Luis Lourenço and José Mourinho

This edition first published in the UK in December 2004 by
Dewi Lewis Media Ltd
8, Broomfield Road
Heaton Moor
Stockport SK4 4ND
www.dewilewismedia.com

>Originally published in Portugal by
Prime Books – Sociedade Editorial, Lda.

>Special collaborators
Jorge Nuno Pinto da Costa and Luís Duque

>Photographs
From the personal archives of José Mourinho
and of the newspapers *A Bola, Record* and *O Jogo*

>Original Design and pagination by
Arco da Velha – Design e Ilustração, Lda.

>Print and binding
Biddles Ltd, Kings Lynn

ISBN: 0-9546843-3-8

12 11 10 9 8 7 6 5 4

The Publishers would like to thank Adam Gumbley for his considerable support and expertise in helping to make this English edition possible.

>> CONTENTS

> INTRODUCTION **MADE IN PORTUGAL** (Page 9)

> CHAPTER I **THE RETURN** (Page 13)

> CHAPTER II **OBJECTIVE ACHIEVED** (Page 25)

> CHAPTER III **THE TRANSITION** (Page 61)

> CHAPTER IV **PREPARING THE FUTURE** (Page 87)

> CHAPTER V **A CLEAN SWEEP** (Page 113)

> CHAPTER VI **ON TOP OF EUROPE** (Page 177)

INTRODUCTION

MADE IN PORTUGAL

Adam Gumbley

November 2004

>> MADE IN PORTUGAL

At the start of the 2003/04 Champions League campaign José Mourinho was asked whether he thought his Porto side could go all the way and attain the ultimate accolade in European club competition. On the surface at least, the question appeared a legitimate one: just four months earlier Porto had triumphed in the UEFA Cup, clinching an unforgettable treble in the process and becoming only the sixth side in history to win their domestic league and cup and the European competition in which they were involved. Yet despite such a glorious campaign, and despite his own inherent self-confidence, the Porto manager dismissed the notion as fanciful. Thoughts of ultimate Champions League glory were reserved for the true giants of European football, the likes of Real Madrid, Juventus and Manchester United. According to Mourinho, and many agreed with him at the time, relative minnows such as FC Porto were merely there to make up the numbers, and pick up some much needed television revenue along the way. Fast-forward nine months and Porto had achieved the unthinkable, the presentation of the European Cup on an unforgettable night in Gelsenkirchen heralding the culmination of a remarkable period of success for *Futebol Clube do Porto*. In just two full seasons as manager in Portugal's second city Mourinho had a trophy haul to rival the lifetime's work of lesser men: two Portuguese league titles, one Portuguese Cup, one UEFA cup and one European Cup. Only a somewhat undeserved defeat at the hands of Benfica in the 2004 Portuguese Cup Final prevented a clean sweep.

Despite his achievements and high profile in his homeland Mourinho arrived in London in the summer of 2004 as something of an enigma. The English press and footballing public were aware of his achievements but somewhat wary of his outlandish statements, mannerisms and demeanour, which they mistook for a moody Latin arrogance. There are many other sides to the personality of *José Mário Santos Mourinho Félix.* Of course, there is evidence of the well-documented self-confidence, bordering on arrogance, which many will feel uncomfortable with, but in this book the reader will encounter additional, perhaps unexpected character traits. Behind the cool, single-minded exterior there is also the dedicated family man; despite the steely determination to succeed in life there is the vulnerability and awareness of the transient nature of the job that every football manager must feel.

As an Englishman working for a Portuguese newspaper, dividing my time between the two countries, I've had the opportunity to observe at first-hand how José Mourinho is perceived in each of these two nations, where for large sections of the population football plays an important part in daily life. In the southeastern corner of Europe his supporters feel an immense debt of gratitude for his labours, while even his detractors show a grudging respect for all he has achieved. Naturally, those supporters of Benfica and Sporting who suffered at Porto's dominance were glad to see the back of him but as the national side thrilled the home nation in Euro 2004 even they were grateful for the way in which Porto's players had developed under his tutelage. Equally, there are those for whom the manner and timing of his departure from FC Porto still rankle but the majority recognise that here was a man who had taken the club as far as he could. The unprecedented cycle of victories that he oversaw at Porto was always going to attract interest from elsewhere and it's natural for those with a sense of ambition in any walk of life to seek out new challenges, and let's be honest, greater financial reward. As Mourinho told journalists in typical style, shortly after his arrival in London, if he had wanted an easy life *"working with the protection of what I have done before"*, he would have remained at Porto, *"beautiful blue chair, the UEFA Champions League trophy, God, and after God, me."* It might be hurtful to admit it in a nation that can support three daily newspapers dedicated to football but the Portuguese game bears no real comparison to the major European leagues. In this respect, perhaps Mourinho's greatest achievement was to restore the Portuguese football, albeit briefly as it now appears, to a position not seen since the glory days of Eusébio's Benfica in the sixties.

As I write, Chelsea have overtaken Arsenal at the top of the Premiership and have already secured their qualification for the latter stages of the Champions League. Of course, there's no guarantee this impressive start will continue but in a matter of months the new man at *The Bridge* has shaped a team with the same stubbornness and obstinacy as Porto, but one with perhaps a little more flair and one that is surely capable of delivering the club's first title after five decades of underachievement. Only time, the grand master, will tell, but today José Mourinho is without doubt the leading young coach in world football. Despite a modest playing career – first with Belenenses and then later with Rio Ave and Sesimbra – here is a man for whom success at some stage in life appeared inevitable. Even when his role was little more than that of an interpreter – imparting the words of wisdom of Sir Bobby Robson, first at Sporting Lisbon and then later at Porto and at Barcelona – it was obvious that his skills were more than merely those of a polyglot.

From an early age Mourinho has lived and breathed the game, cultivating his studious approach, learning first from his father, whose own coaching career spanned almost twenty years, and later in a more formal environment with a degree in Sports Science from *ISEF* – a Lisbon University. This background goes some way to explaining his coaching methodology and meticulous preparation for matches. It brought him success as an assistant coach under Robson and Van Gaal but, as Mourinho himself admits, he was a frustrated assistant and it was only a matter of time before he sought out greater responsibility. This came first with Benfica, but to his eternal credit Mourinho had the strength and conviction to walk away when it became clear the club could not match his own ambition. A spell with União de Leiria followed, not one of Portugal's traditional greats and undoubtedly a backward step at the time but one that would ultimately prove necessary for greater successes down the line. Clearly, Mourinho possessed the requisite humility to drop down a level, confident that his time would come, and the opportunity soon presented itself. In January 2002 Mourinho was appointed manager of FC Porto and promptly announced *"next season we'll be champions"*. As one *Portista* told me, everything you needed to know about José Mourinho's conviction and sense of ambition was encapsulated in that one phrase. As we now know not only did he keep his promise, he delivered much more besides.

Today José Mourinho combines the man-management skills of the likes of Sir Alex Ferguson with the meticulous, studious approach of the likes of Arsène Wenger. He displays the charisma and motivational skills of a born leader and combines it with the scholarly attentiveness of the most dedicated of students. There is another interesting paradox – here is a man who succeeds in being the players' confidante, in fostering an unbreakable team spirit and group culture, but at the same time manages to maintain a healthy distance and ensure that even the most egocentric of the modern game's pampered superstars are fully aware of who's in charge. It is these ingredients, this mixture of charismatic leadership and painstaking attention to detail, that combine to make José Mourinho the outstanding coach of his generation.

As he starts to build his empire at Chelsea, this book looks back on Mourinho's formative years as a manager in Portugal, focusing on the triumphs and setbacks that moulded his managerial style and shaped his footballing philosophy. *José Mourinho – Made In Portugal.*

Adam Gumbley
English Correspondent, *A Bola*
London, November 2004

>> CHAPTER I **THE RETURN**

BARCELONA, JUNE 2000

A TOUGH FINAL YEAR

THE ASSISTANT COACH NO MORE

THE MASTERS: ROBSON AND VAN GAAL

HOLIDAYS AND... UNEMPLOYMENT

>> CHAPTER 1 **THE RETURN**

Sitges is a small tourist town, some 20 kilometres from Barcelona, capital of Catalonia. In May 1996, José Mourinho, along with Bobby Robson, joined Barcelona Football Club, and when the club's directors suggested he live in Sitges, in a magnificent duplex by the sea, he didn't hesitate. The town reminded him of Setúbal, the city where he was born and where he had always lived. Just like the capital of the Sado, the sea also bathes Sitges. It would be a good place to adapt to a new country, and he would find it easier to remember his origins as he looked out out to sea, over the white sandy beaches. Sitges, like Setúbal, also has its esplanades and cafés stretching along the coast, as well as fresh fish and seafood – and that typical summer atmosphere that begins as early as May. Most importantly, though, it is only twenty minutes from Barcelona, but is still a quiet country town, at least in winter. A relaxing place where you can find much needed relief from stress – much like Setúbal, a good place to live.

Four years later, on a hot summer's day in June, we drove slowly along Sitges' long and narrow coastal road. Halfway along, José Mourinho stopped his black Volvo cabriolet, parked and slowly got out of the car. It was early, and although the journey ahead was long, there was time to bid one last farewell to the friends he'd made as soon as he arrived in Catalonia.

Among the first people he'd met in Sitges were the Mattas. They had got on well immediately and their friendship had grown steadily. It grew even stronger when his wife Tami, who was five months pregnant at the time, joined Mourinho. Moving to another country, even one so close to Portugal, is never easy and the Mattas family understood that they could play a role in this new chapter – which they did, to perfection. Five brothers and a sister, the Mattas run several family businesses in Spain. If one of the family wasn't around, there was always another to count on – or the wife or one of the children of the various couples. So, even when José Mourinho was away at training camp, or when Barcelona played abroad, Tami never felt alone.

Javi Mattas stood at the entrance to the *Sports Bar*. It was as if he'd guessed that his Portuguese friend had arrived. We went in, had coffee, and read the headlines of the Barcelona sports newspapers. Not once did any of us mention the past or the future, football or Barcelona. We made small talk – nothing emotional.

> A TOUGH FINAL YEAR

We then set off on the long journey back to Setúbal. As we were leaving Sitges, I watched José Mourinho. I always have an uncontrollable urge to look back, to try to capture an image of any place I go to, as I believe I'll be able to hold onto it and remember it later. I thought that after four years of living in Sitges, José Mourinho would do the same. I was wrong. Unperturbed by anything, my travelling companion just paid careful attention to the road ahead. As always, he was waiting for me to strike up conversation. I usually choose the topics and talk, while he listens and says little. It's been this way through decades of solid friendship; I'm the speaker, he's the listener.

His time at Barcelona had very nearly come to an end a year before. In the close season of 1999, various clubs had invited Mourinho to be head coach. The most attractive offer had come from Sporting de Braga. I was one of the people who dissuaded him from accepting, and I can well remember my reasoning: *"What can you expect if you go? You might get fired six months from now, as so often happens in Portuguese football. You've got nothing to gain, but much to lose. Here in Barcelona, you have a fantastic life, you learn a lot from great masters and great players, you have no pressure in terms of winning or losing, you live in a wonderful city, and you're making good money. At 38, you should stay here and enjoy the good life God is giving you."*

However, his last year in Barcelona had proved to be difficult. Even today, I'm still not sure if my advice was the best a friend could give; my only consolation is that I wasn't the only one to think this way. Relatives, including his own father, and other friends also advised José Mourinho to stay in Spain.

He wasn't happy that final year – the last year in which he worked with Louis Van Gaal – neither personally, nor professionally. He later confided in me that he'd been *"a frustrated coach"* during that period. He went on to explain that he'd stayed in Spain because he would earn more money there than if he had come to Portugal as a head coach, and so he could continue to give his family a fantastic quality of life. But, above all, he stayed on at Barcelona because his hopes were still set on the only trophy he hadn't yet won as assistant coach: the Champions League.

As assistant coach in Portugal he'd won two Leagues, a Cup and two Super Cups; while in Spain he'd won two Leagues, two King's Cups, two Super Cups, a Cup Winners Cup, and a European Super Cup. However, he dreamed of winning the Champions League, and he knew for certain that 1999 would be his last year with Barcelona. A man of strong conviction, José Mourinho believed it was possible for him to help bring Barcelona the ultimate glory for a football club, and so he decided to stay.

A year later, he received the same advice, except that the decision to leave Barcelona had already been taken. This time, nothing would stop Mourinho from following the path he had set out for himself. All the advice in the world would not sway him, and those closest to him realised that Zé Mário was not open to talking, discussing or even exchanging any thoughts on this matter. Now, some years later, he still praises his wife for always standing by him then, both as companion and friend.

I was an anguished assistant coach, somewhat harsh, even overly critical, I'd say

"Tami was always there and she witnessed the moments of anguish I went through that final year. She kept up with everything and understood what I was going through. I would often get home and act more like a critic than an assistant coach. During the day I would work at Nou Camp, the serious and faithful assistant I'd always been. At home I was far more critical, often thinking about how Van Gaal had taken this one off and put that one on, whereas I would have done this and that. So, I was already an anguished assistant coach, somewhat harsh, even overly critical, I'd say. This situation made me realise that my time there was over. Tami understood this perfectly because she saw and lived with my dramas, doubts and anguish. It was she who always stood at my side and supported me in a decision that was by no means easy, but which seemed inevitable."

And inevitable it was. Furthermore, Louis Van Gaal, who'd trained Barcelona for three years also left the club, as did the president, Josep Luís Nuñez. It wasn't a good season for a club that was used to winning everything, even though their European dream only came to an end in the semi-finals against Valencia.

A replacement for Nuñez was found a few months before the end of the Spanish league season, when the *blau-grana* members elected a man that Mourinho knew and respected, but who, he felt, did not have the same leadership capacity as his predecessor. That man was the former vice-president, Joan Gaspart. With Van Gaal gone and the season over, the Spaniard Serra Ferrer, who'd come from Barcelona's *cantera*, was, after some hesitation, chosen as head coach. If Mourinho had been a little indifferent to the first decision, he disagreed with the second. With another year left, he rescinded his contract. He did not believe Barcelona would succeed with Serra Ferrer at the helm.

With Sitges now behind us, the Volvo glided along the wide, well-kept Spanish motorways. If we kept up a good speed, nine hours of travelling lay ahead. José Mourinho's last journey in the Barcelona chapter. I remember having accompanied him that first day, him and Bobby Robson, when they'd set off to sign their contract. Four years later, with his family and belongings already back in Setúbal, I now accompanied him on his last day, when he'd gone to pick up the only thing he'd left in Barcelona – his car. José Mourinho left as he had arrived. No fanfare and no drama.

> ASSISTANT COACH NO MORE

Portugal was the destination – unemployment the immediate future. I asked him if he was at all certain about what he'd find in Portugal, given he had been away for so long. I wanted to know if he remembered that in Portugal it was almost impossible to remain coach of a club for four years running. I was sure that Mourinho's difficult life as a coach hadn't yet begun. The hard Portuguese reality and an uncertain future were – and still are – a sad reality for the coaches who worked – and who work – in Portugal. Up until now, Mourinho had led a life free from great pressure, with someone with more responsibility above him. And apart from a brief time with Estrela da Amadora, as Manuel Fernandes' assistant, he'd only worked with big clubs in Portugal – clubs like Sporting and Porto, which always provide some peace of mind. He'd only known a good life. Difficult days were yet to come… and most certainly would.

His answers to my questions came as no surprise. Mourinho had been away from Portuguese football, but he wasn't out of touch with what was happening. Eyes fixed firmly on the road ahead, he began to tell me what he thought his life would be like in the near future.

"I know it'll be a struggle. I'm going to an environment where I might not feel very comfortable because the mentality is already a little different. Apart from that, I'm also aware that I don't belong to the 'clan', to those who deal the cards and set up the game, if you know what I mean. Naturally, taking all of this into account, I feel a little alien. Plus, I was never a successful player, so I won't enjoy the protection that many others do; I won't have a successful past as a footballer to back me up."

Nevertheless, José Mourinho returned to Portugal under no real pressure. Although he knew he faced unemployment, as all the coaching positions had been taken, he wasn't afraid of the future. He'd managed to build up a tidy little nest egg in Barcelona, enough to allow him to be without a job for some time until he found another club. And he had limitless faith in himself.

"I'm not the least bit afraid of the future. I have great confidence in myself and in my knowledge. I know that I can make the difference and that I can win."

> THE MASTERS: ROBSON AND VAN GAAL

In his self-analysis, he clearly understood and identified the coach he had been when he left Portugal, and the coach he had become after his time with Barcelona. The experiences gained at *Nou Camp* were an endless source of knowledge, both in terms of theory and practice. His two great masters had contributed a great deal in this regard.

On the one hand, there was Bobby Robson, a man who *'lived and breathed the pitch'*. As he was above all a coach on the pitch, he left all the homework to Mourinho – the planning and the preparation. On the other hand, there was the Dutchman Louis Van Gaal, with a very different style to Robson's. He was methodical and planned everything right down to the very last detail, leaving all the work on the pitch to his assistants. This basic difference in approach between the two trainers was of vital importance to Mourinho as he studied, understood, developed and put into practice both elements, which are essential when coaching and preparing a football team: planning and action. That's precisely what he did.

Mourinho explained how he evolved under Bobby Robson's method.

"Bobby Robson isn't interested in studying, systematising or planning the training practice. He is a pitch man; he's about training and having direct contact with the players. He's also an attacking coach. If we were to divide the match into three parts, we'd see that Bobby Robson's work concentrates mainly on the final part – finishing, scoring. That's his focus, and this is the area that he prioritises. In this case, I tried to take a step back – that is, whilst maintaining the primacy of attacking football, I tried to organise it better, and this organisation stems directly from the defence."

Then he spoke of Louis Van Gaal.

"With Van Gaal I could arrive at the stadium a mere half an hour before

the practice. I had nothing to worry about because the work was always completely defined. I knew everything we were going to do beforehand. From the practice objectives to the time for doing exercises, not forgetting the main points of methodology, nothing was left to chance and everything was programmed in great detail. All that was left for me – and for the other assistants in the different areas – was the training on the pitch. This meant that my work improved tremendously in terms of quality because, as I mentioned, with Robson I didn't get much practice as a coach on the pitch."

But in addition to everything that these two men taught him, Mourinho had yet another extremely important source of knowledge: the players at Barcelona – some of the best professionals in the world – where stars such as Ronaldo, Rivaldo, Figo, Guardiola, Stoichkov and Kluivert shone. Of these, all had won the FIFA Golden Ball, with the exception of Pep Guardiola and Patrick Kluivert.

"You can't help but learn when you coach players of this calibre – you even learn about human relationships. Players at this level don't accept what they're told simply because of the authority of the person who's saying it. We have to show them that we're right. Here, the old story of 'the Mister[1] *is always right' does not apply. In fact, it generally isn't applicable, and even less so with highly developed players, which is the case with any Barcelona player. The relationship I had with them taught me one of my main virtues as a coach. The tactical work I encourage isn't about there being a 'transmitter' on the one hand and a 'receptor' on the other. I call it the 'guided discovery'; that is they discover according to my clues. I construct practice situations that will set them on a certain path. They begin to sense this, so we talk, discuss things and come to a conclusion. But for this to work, the players we coach must have their own opinions. I would often stop the practice and ask them what they were feeling at a certain moment. For example, they'd tell me that they thought the right back was too far away from the centre back. Ok, let's bring them closer to each other and see how that works. We'd try this out two or three times, and I'd ask them again what they thought. This is the way it*

I have well-defined plans, ambitions and objectives

1. *In Portugal, football players and those involved in football usually refer to the head coach as 'Mister'.*

worked, until all of us came to a conclusion. This methodology is what I call the 'guided discovery'."

Mourinho was now much more of an all-round coach and had more knowledge than when he had left FC Porto and Portugal. This could be seen clearly – at least in his opinion, and in the opinion of someone who had always supported him: Tami. However, would this be enough to embark safely on a career as a head coach?

Although he believed in himself wholeheartedly, he didn't set his sights very high, as he didn't have overly high expectations regarding the future.

"Sooner or later, I believe it is possible to find a smaller club in Portugal. I've already received an offer from Sporting de Braga in the past, and I think this is the mark for me. I have a project to present to whoever wants to hire me; I have well-defined ambitions and objectives. I have a document outlining my direction, which will guarantee my work. Also, if Barcelona has given me anything – and it has surely given me a great deal – it is exposure in my own country. Having been Barcelona's assistant coach, I ended up doing many interviews, and this has made it possible for many people to get to know me, my ideas, what I think about the game. That is another trump card I take from Catalonia in order to start working in Portugal. Whoever wants to hire me is already somewhat familiar with my work, so I am not completely unknown. It won't be a complete shot in the dark because they know what I want; the only thing they don't know is whether I can put my ideas into practice. Anyway, I don't want to think about that now. What I want to do, and will do, when I get to Portugal, is go on holiday with my family".

Finally, after almost a full day of travelling, we arrived in Setúbal at around nine in the evening. The sun hadn't yet set. I live very close to José Mourinho; he dropped me off and we bid each other a solemn *"see you tomorrow"*.

> HOLIDAYS AND... UNEMPLOYMENT

Ferragudo is a small village close to Portimão, on the Algarve. José Mourinho's father, 65-year-old José Manuel Mourinho Félix, was born here, and Zé Mário has always chosen Ferragudo as one of his favourite holiday destinations. The beach, the small central square where everyone meets at the end of the day, and the town's proximity to Portimão and Praia da Rocha, all make it the ideal spot for those who like to stay in the Algarve – surrounded by peace and quiet yet only a stone's throw from 'civilisation'. A few months earlier, José Mourinho had bought a holiday home there. It was exactly what he needed. He was unemployed for the first time and Ferragudo was just the place to be. Far away from everyone, Mourinho wanted only three things: to be with his family, to rest, and to study. And that's what he did.

Whether in Ferragudo, or in Setúbal, he calmly set about studying and keeping himself up-to-date. He read all the books on football that he could lay his hands on, he searched the Internet for texts and websites – for anything new. He watched hundreds of videos and DVDs, and, at the same time, he dedicated himself to his family. At that time, there was already a second child – José Mário, who'd been born six months earlier in Barcelona. Tita, his daughter, was now four years old. For the first time, José Mourinho had time for his children – something new for him. But it wouldn't be so for much longer.

In the meantime, the pre-season began for the 18 teams that were to kick off the 2000/2001 Portuguese season. Contrary to what he usually did, Mourinho didn't go to the stadiums, except for one.

"I didn't watch a single match at stadiums, except for those played in the Bonfim Stadium. I was in a tricky situation and I couldn't, nor did I want to be misinterpreted. Everyone knows that I have always supported Vitória de Setúbal. I've been a member since the day I was born, and the Bonfim Stadium was my second home during my childhood. So I knew I could go there with my friends, without giving rise to any speculation. Also, Vitória had slipped into the Second League, and everyone knew that the second division wasn't in my plans."

It was also around this time that Mourinho drew up his 'Bible'. A document that no one has access to, and which 'steers' his professional life.

"I remember the date well because it was the first time in my life that I had ever had a holiday at that time of the year. It was in August that I drew up a document that has never been and never will be published. It's my 'training file', where I keep all the 'directives' for my work. It contains the objectives and methodologies for my practice, and how to achieve these; that is, 'for these objectives, use those exercises'. In fact, this document is nothing more than the systematic setting down of my ideas. If I had to give it a title, it would be 'The evolution of my training concepts'. In 1990 I didn't think about training the way I did in 2000. For example, when I was with Sporting I learnt a lot about fitness training from two great professionals, Roger Spry and Terziisky. But in my approach today there is no room for the traditional fitness trainer. Priorities have changed over the years. So, I have got into the habit of taking down notes every day, be they related to training, or simply my own thoughts. Since I began my career, even back in my time at Estrela da Amadora with Manuel Fernandes, I have always put everything down in writing at the end of every practice. In fact, it was the collection of all these notes that gave rise to the file I mentioned. After I had drawn it up, I was definitely ready to be a coach."

In my methodology today, there is no room for the traditional fitness trainer

Patience is one of José Mourinho's qualities, and he stands by the old adage *'patience is a virtue'*. He arrived back in Portugal ready to wait. He had convinced himself that, with luck, he would find a club by December. It's well-known that the Christmas period is a difficult barrier to overcome for the coaches of badly ranked teams. In football, bad luck for some usually means good luck for others – not only on, but also off the pitch. José Mourinho was prepared to wait his turn, so much so that during this period, from June to September, he even turned down an offer from England. Added to patience, he has another virtue: perseverance. Mourinho had decided his objective and he wouldn't rest until he'd achieved it. This helps us to understand why he turned down an offer from Newcastle.

"I must admit that it was a little difficult to be unemployed in September. I saw the others heading off to training camp and I was at home; the others had matches on Sundays and I'd watch them on television. It was a little difficult for me; it was the first time since I had started working that I was unemployed.

One day, the phone rang; it was Bobby Robson. He knew my ambition would no longer allow me to accept any post as an assistant coach; nevertheless that was the offer he had for me. Since he suspected that I wouldn't accept it, he told me it would be only for a year, two tops, and that at the end of that time I would be the head coach, and he club manager. But Bobby Robson had forgotten that I had worked with him for many years, and so I knew him well. He is a man who will only leave the pitch when he stops working. It is unthinkable to picture him as a manager of any club, watching the practices and the games from the stands. I didn't take him up on his offer, knowing that sooner or later my time would come."

>> CHAPTER II **OBJECTIVE ACHIEVED**

BENFICA 2000/01

"TONI IS BENFICA'S NEW COACH"
A 'BUNCH' OF PLAYERS
"I'LL CARRY ON REGARDLESS"
A 'GHOST' NAMED SANCHEZ
THE 'GRAPESHOT BROTHERS'
THE TURNING POINT
VILARINHO DEFEATS VALE E AZEVEDO
THE SABRY CASE
A SQUAD SPLIT DOWN THE MIDDLE
LAST MATCH AS BENFICA'S COACH
IT'S ALL OR NOTHING

>> CHAPTER II **OBJECTIVE ACHIEVED**

The phone rang a lot sooner than he had expected. It was mid September – and dinner time. As he did every day since he'd been on 'enforced' holiday, José Mourinho was having dinner with his family. He was at his Setúbal home when Tami handed him the phone. *"It's for you."* Already at the table, José Mourinho stretched out his arm and took the call. Little did he know how it was to change his life.

The previous day Benfica had played Estrela da Amadora on match-day five of the First Division. The score was 2-1, but the 'reds' [2] had been losing almost up to the end. Every day there were more and more protests about the coach, Jupp Heynckes, and the team's weak performance was the last straw. The president at the time, Vale e Azevedo, had taken the decision to dismiss the German coach and – to everyone's surprise – Mourinho was chosen to replace him.

"The person who called me was my great friend Eládio Paramés, a former journalist for 'A Bola' [3]*, who was the Director of Communications at Benfica/SAD* [4] *at the time. He asked me to go to Lisbon and we had an interesting conversation.*

'Zé, Mr Vale e Azevedo would like to speak to you tonight. He has an offer to make you. Can you be in Lisbon in the next few hours?'

'You're mad. Don't even think it. You all know I won't go back to being an assistant coach, so going there would be a waste of time! Please apologise to the President, but tell him I won't go there for nothing, because I've made up my mind not to be an assistant again, and there's no going back on that.'

'Come on. Come to Lisbon and talk to him. The offer isn't for an assistant coach. Get in your car and get here.'

'It isn't for an assistant? Then tell me, what do you guys want?'

'I'm saying no more. We'll speak when you get here.'"

Unruffled, but pensive, José Mourinho hung up the phone and tucked into his dinner. He thought about an incident from the year before, during the 1999/2000 close season. He'd been in Spain when the phone rang. It had been

2. *Red is the colour worn by Benfica.*
3. *A Portuguese sports newspaper mainly dedicated to football.*
4. *SAD: Sociedade Anónima Desportiva – a public limited company (football club).*

Vale e Azevedo. The Benfica president had just signed Jupp Heynckes for a two-year period, and he was in Barcelona to complete his new coaching team. He wanted Mourinho to be 'the' assistant coach and had offered him a four-year contract.

It had been an easy decision: *"I won't go from being Barcelona's assistant coach to Benfica's assistant coach. Also, I once said in an interview that I would only return to Portugal to work as the head coach."*

José Mourinho had thanked him and Vale e Azevedo had returned to Benfica's Luz Stadium [5] without an assistant coach for Jupp Heynckes. Would history repeat itself?

> "TONI IS BENFICA'S NEW COACH"

Usually the drive from Setúbal to Lisbon takes about half an hour. José Mourinho turned on the radio and left it on the station it was tuned to. Halfway into the journey he heard the news: *"Toni is Benfica's new coach."*

His first thoughts were, *"Eládio made me leave home to go to Lisbon at this late hour for nothing. I'll have to tell them that I won't be an assistant to either Toni, or Fábio Capello. I won't be anybody's assistant."* He picked up his mobile and called Eládio Paramés. José Mourinho had barely heard the voice on the other end of the line when he launched into his attack. *"Toni is going to Benfica and I'm going to turn right round and not even go there. You know I won't be an assistant coach any longer."*

His time as head coach had come!

Eládio Paramés knew Mourinho well and that he was as good as his word, so he had to lay his cards on the table: *"Take it easy. The president has sworn me to secrecy, but the way you're putting it, I have no choice but to tell you. You are going to be offered the post of Benfica's head coach."* That was exactly what Mourinho needed to hear to persuade him to continue his journey.

5. *Luz – the name of the Benfica Stadium, is taken from the area in which the stadium is located.*

When he arrived in Lisbon, Eládio Paramés was waiting for him, along with Álvaro Braga Júnior, Executive Director of Benfica/SAD, and Michel Preud'Homme, Benfica's Sports Director. The four set off for one of Vale e Azevedo's homes in the centre of the city.

It was a little after midnight. The Benfica president shook his hand firmly at the door. Pragmatic as always, Vale e Azevedo got down to business as soon as they had sat down. *"Do you want to be Benfica's coach?"*

Mourinho said yes – though this wasn't his final answer. Apart from contract-related issues, there was still a lot to discuss. He had never gone into any project without first knowing all the details. He wanted to know what plans Vale e Azevedo had for the club's future; what investments he'd be willing to make in the short-term; and, finally, how far he was willing to go so that the club could return to those glorious times that stood as landmarks in its history. He also wanted to know what expectations the president had of the future coach.

José Mourinho heard one of the most unexpected answers he'd ever been given in the world of football. Vale e Azevedo stated that he didn't know anything about football, but boasted of his astuteness when it came to assessing people's character and personality. After listening to Preud'Homme, Paramés and Álvaro Braga, he'd had no difficulty choosing José Mourinho to succeed Jupp Heynckes.

Mourinho listened to Vale e Azevedo's plans. The president wanted to 'Portuguesify' the club with a young team, using many Portuguese players from the club's junior ranks. Essentially, it came down to seeking success, but with no money. This wasn't exactly an unusual idea, but the only viable one for Benfica, as it was going through one of the greatest crises in its history. As well as a financial crisis, there was a sporting crisis. José Mourinho had been chosen to perform a 'miracle'.

They came to a consensus. Benfica would invest in training, José Mourinho would be given time to work, and no titles would be expected of him, at least not in the short-term.

Elections at Benfica had already been fixed, and Vale e Azevedo offered the coach a six-month contract, which would bind him to the club up until the end of the 2000/2001 season. However, there was a clause that the contract would automatically be renewed for a further two years should Vale e Azevedo

win the elections. And so they agreed on the idea of *"time to work while investing in the young"*.

José Mourinho had walked into Vale e Azevedo's house unemployed, he walked out as the Benfica coach.

Not bad for someone who had wanted to set off on a coaching career. José Mourinho became the youngest-ever Portuguese coach at Benfica – only Sven-Goran Eriksson had been younger than him. At 37, he felt he could do something different at Benfica, something positive. The club hadn't won any titles in recent seasons, and its members, used to winning, were thirsty for victory. Fully confident of his own abilities, like no other, José Mourinho believed that his time as head coach had now come.

He arrived home half an hour later. He woke up Tami saying, *"I'm going to coach Benfica, and tomorrow I'm off to Lisbon, to any hotel for two or three days, because I need to concentrate solely on this."* His wife turned over and went back to sleep. José Mourinho also slept soundly that night.

> A "BUNCH" OF PLAYERS

The next day, Wednesday, was the squad's day off. The new Benfica trainer got up early, packed a small bag, switched off his mobile phone, and said goodbye to his family. For the next few days, he was heading into a self-imposed reclusion. On Thursday, he would coach the team for the very first time. During those days, his life would be divided between the Stadium and the hotel, constantly working. José Mourinho believed it was possible to do a good job at the Luz Stadium. In the meantime, however, the reality at Benfica, wouldn't allow the new coach to set his sights very high.

"I made an analysis and came to the conclusion that I was faced with a badly ranked team, made up of old or foreign players of dubious quality, not to say bad quality players. In short, it was a weak squad with no future and no ambition. It was a team that was used to losing, and wasn't too worried about this. The players worked little and didn't really care. For these reasons, I didn't feel that Benfica had a squad. What it had was a 'bunch' of players who'd been signed haphazardly. It was a completely unbalanced group. Looking to the future, only Meira, Marchena, Enke and Van Hooijdonk were fully prepared to play in a real Benfica. Then, there was a group with quality, but no motivation. And finally, we had the junior group, with all the qualities and flaws of youth. Here we had footballers like Miguel, Geraldo, João Tomás, Carlitos, Diogo Luís and Maniche, players who needed tactical work to develop and to assert themselves. This was the Benfica I found."

The 'stars' were Enke, Poborsky and Van Hooidjonk – but above all, the Egyptian, Sabry, who'd so impressed the Benfica fans after leading Benfica to victory over Sporting at the Alvalade Stadium the previous season, with a goal close to the end. However, José Mourinho felt that Sabry had talent, but didn't fit in with the team and had no group culture.

"I knew immediately that it would be difficult for Sabry to be successful with me. There weren't many talented players, and so I had to make the group work as a block, as a whole – that would be its strong point. Sabry never managed to adapt to that structure, and I would never abdicate from group cohesion in favour of one person."

Aware of the reality, José Mourinho clearly understood that it was to be a season for only 'managing'. Preparation for the next season would have to start at once. And so his only immediate objective was to minimise the havoc the present season would surely bring.

Feeling positive, Mourinho found in Benfica a 'rearguard' of friendly people. Paramés, Álvaro Braga and Preud'Homme formed a united group, with a common plan for Benfica. José Mourinho was confident he would never have any problems with this group. The day Vale e Azevedo left the club after losing the elections, he himself said, *"It's a shame that when I won the elections this group wasn't already formed and working with me."*

In the meantime though, another group was put together: the technical team. When choosing an assistant coach, Mourinho was asked if he would be taking anyone with him. He had said no, and that he would be interested in someone who already knew Benfica. So, they drew up a profile: an ex-Benfica player, with a strong personality and charisma. Someone remembered Mozer, to which José Mourinho replied, *"I don't know him personally, but I admit he fits the jigsaw perfectly. As far as I'm concerned, I don't mind if it's Mozer."*

As for the rest of the technical staff, from the Spanish fitness trainer, Angel Vilda (to whom Mourinho is always quick to pay the greatest compliments), through to the Observation Department, and the Medical Department, the new trainer accepted them all, with no reservations. Benfica could not afford to spend more than was strictly necessary and José Mourinho accepted the club's 'financial debility'. Besides, he had nothing against the names presented. He assumed that if they were Benfica professionals, they'd surely have quality. He was wrong, as we will see.

> *"I'LL CARRY ON REGARDLESS"*

Meanwhile, José Mourinho began to come in for some flack in the papers, on the radio and on the television. Many commentators and journalists, as well as former players and others involved in the game, questioned his lack of experience, as well as his competence to hold so high a post. These harbingers of misfortune failed to notice that the more they attacked the Benfica coach, the greater the empathy between the club's members and Mourinho. Without realising it, they were doing him a favour.

Mourinho started off at Benfica under fire, but as always he remained unruffled. *"I'll carry on regardless,"* was his motto. Without getting worked up, and above all without letting himself be intimidated, he began his work with the club. He paid no heed to the criticisms – nor does he today – and he still refuses to name those who wanted to put an end to his career as a coach just as it was starting. In a way, José Mourinho was still paying the price for having been overly direct in an interview he'd given to one of the Portuguese sports papers in Barcelona. In it he'd questioned Portuguese football in general, and the work methods used by Portuguese coaches in particular. Many never forgave him for such 'audacity', while others never forgot his supreme brashness in criticising the 'perfect world'.

But his path was set out. The suspicions and attacks only gave him more strength to carry on. And within Benfica, there was a wonderful atmosphere, where Mourinho found the peace of mind he needed to carry out the work he was planning and intended to see through.

On the first day of practice at Luz Stadium, Mourinho arrived two hours before practice. *"I always like to arrive at least an hour before training begins. I have never been late in my life. There are always things to take care of and people to speak to. In the first place, I always like to be the first to arrive; then I like to inspect the length of the grass and see if it needs to be watered; I speak to the people in charge of the equipment I need for the practice – portable goals, cones, balls, etc.; I have to draw up a sketch for the layout of the equipment on the pitch; I meet with the Medical Department to find out about the players' physical condition – who can train unconditionally, whose training is restricted and by what, so that we can adopt a more appropriate training session for them; I also like to look through the papers. I always have many tasks to carry out before the beginning of any practice. For all these reasons, I always arrive much earlier than anyone else."*

It was then that José Mourinho felt like the Benfica coach. In his tracksuit, bearing the eagle [6] motif, he knew there was no turning back. The moment he'd always waited for, and for which he had prepared for years, had finally arrived. Whilst he knew that difficult times lay ahead, for now he was living his dream.

"The first days at a football club are always perfect and the players are totally receptive. They're always available, they're all punctual. They work

6. *The eagle is the symbol of Benfica.*

hard, they collaborate and talk – everything runs like clockwork. Aware of this reality, I decided to observe more at the beginning, rather than intervene. There were two days left before the match with Boavista, and little to be done. Even before we started training, I had spoken to the squad in the changing rooms for the first time. It wasn't a long speech, and that may be why I started to 'win them over' there and then. The group began to take shape at that moment, and there were only two possibilities: you were either on the boat, or off it. I made them two promises. The first was my guarantee of 'quality work', with which they themselves would improve, both on an individual and collective level. The other promise was that I would be 'direct'. I knew that Benfica was a club that was influenced by information, counter-information, rumour and gossip. As I couldn't promise to 'armour plate' the Football Department, I told them I would be completely direct. In this way, I wanted them to be sure that no matter what decisions the coach took in relation to Benfica players, they would always be the first to know, and they'd know it from me. I wanted the group to be a little more closed off from the outside, and for there to be greater solidarity inside the group. I was convinced that the Media should not be a means of communication among people in Benfica, and that it should only carry out its role to inform. This was only possible with a 'direct' approach, and so the door to my office would always be open to any of the professionals in Benfica. I said nothing more and we went onto the pitch to train for the first time."

There were only two possibilities: you were either on the boat or off it

Vale e Azevedo and the vice-president, José Manuel Capristano, also heard this speech. The Benfica president then addressed the players and confirmed that José Mourinho had the Board's total confidence for the next two and a half years.

The next day, Thursday, 21 September, the front pages of the sports newspapers all spoke of Manuel Vilarinho. With elections around a month away, the man who was to succeed Vale e Azevedo as Benfica president, unreservedly stated, *"Toni is my coach"*. This made headlines, but the message didn't end there. In the paper *A Bola*, Vilarinho was even clearer. *"José*

Mourinho knows he is not my coach and, as he is a man of good faith, he will agree to resign." The gauntlet had been thrown down and José Mourinho immediately understood the rules of the game. With Vale e Azevedo he'd stay in Benfica for two and a half years. With Vilarinho he'd be there for little over a month.

> A 'GHOST' NAMED SANCHEZ

José Mourinho's first match with Benfica took place on a Saturday night, on 23 September 2000, at the Bessa Stadium, against Boavista. The team chose a hotel in Espinho for their training. It was here that Mourinho experienced one of the most absurd episodes during his time with Benfica.

"I asked the club's Observation Department for a thorough analysis of our opponent. So, I waited for a detailed analysis of Boavista: their key features, the way they played, their strong and weak points, a profile of the players, their qualities and flaws, etc. Nothing special, given the greatness of a club like Benfica and its levels of professionalism.

When I looked at the report they'd given me, I found a team made up of only ten players. It's true. According to what they handed me, their drawings and tactical analysis, Boavista played with only ten players. The absent player was 'only' Sanchez, one of the team's most influential players. I thought, 'What have I got myself into? How is this possible?' Obviously, I never asked Benfica's Observation Department for a single report ever again."

José Mourinho immediately met with Álvaro Braga Júnior and told him it wasn't possible to work with 'that' Observation Department. He was later told that after the elections he could remodel whichever departments he wanted to, and so Mourinho waited. However, he did not work with the Observation Department ever again. Instead he hired an old university colleague, whom he paid out of his own pocket, to carry out the work that any department in any smaller club should do.

And so it was in this strange and confusing 'red' world – very different to Barcelona – that José Mourinho continued to prepare for the match against Boavista. In his final address before the match, he felt once more that he had before him a group of unmotivated men with little self-confidence. He asked

each of them, individually, if they played internationally. He got the same reply from everyone: *"Yes, I play for my country's national team."* How was it possible then to have a team of international players in that psychological frame of mind? His speech was more or less as follows: *"You all have to play more than you have done, you all have potential for more, you're internationals, we have to be winners, etc, etc, etc."* Essentially, he 'massaged' the players' egos so as to increase their confidence a little.

It turned out to be a match to forget; they lost 1-0. In the history of football, José Mourinho may well be the coach who has suffered the earliest goal in his career; sixty seconds was all it took. Worse still, it was a Boavista move that Mourinho had foreseen.

"In my talks before the match, I always define some typical situations set up by the opponents; that is, the moves they usually try out, those they have studied. When Boavista were on the attack, they mainly relied on the flanks for crosses and diagonals near the post. Before the match started, I warned the Benfica players about these situations over and over again. And sure enough, in Boavista's first attacking move there was a cross near the post, which went in and gave them their goal. I thought to myself, 'What type of player is Rojas? Does he understand Portuguese, or do I have to speak in Spanish for him to understand me?' That's when I began to realise that there were players in Benfica who, because of their mindset, or shall we say attitude, could not play for us."

Benfica came nowhere close to a draw. They didn't manage to create any goal-scoring opportunities, but neither did they come close to losing by any more goals.

José Mourinho came to the conclusion that the Benfica players lacked a work ethic.

Van Hooijdonk was perhaps the most striking personality in that working group

"Much of the internal friction stemmed from the fact that they worked little. For example, Van Hooijdonk was regarded as problematic. As far as I'm concerned, his problem was that he wanted to win and taste success. Given his past experience in other leagues, he knew that only work leads to success. He clearly understood that he could not win without quality work, without a strong team, or without all the players being equally ambitious. His conflicts with some team-mates arose from this awareness.

My working methods, which were immediately reflected in the training momentum and which were in line with what Van Hooijdonk thought, put an end to all his problems. He was, perhaps, the most striking personality in that working group."

> THE 'GRAPESHOT BROTHERS'

It will be useful, then, to take a look at Benfica's daily routine on the pitch at Luz Stadium.

"There were always, at least, four or five players, who didn't train. They didn't train because they'd injured themselves a little during the previous day's work, or because they were suffering from muscular fatigue, and this would force them to rest the next day. This situation arose from the close relationship between them and the Medical Department, and so I was tied hand and foot.

Then there was the question of aggressiveness during practice, which was non-existent. Some people simply didn't want there to be the slightest aggressiveness during training. So they trained without shin-guards, and obviously without any contact or competitive situations. At the very least, practice at Benfica was ridiculous. Every day, a group of nice guys would kick the ball about a bit, and do some running – that was it.

The first thing I did to change this, was to involve players from the B team. I asked for Diogo Luís, Geraldo and Nuno Abreu, 'poor players' who were earning 750 Euros a month. Young players who wanted to train with the 'stars', and who were highly competitive and motivated – so much so that after a few days they were immediately known as the 'Grapeshot Brothers'. In an extremely objective way, and as a result of the aggressiveness they imposed, these three young players modified the competitive situations and, in a certain way, the mindset of all the others. As for me, I made some changes, not in terms of methodology, but in relation to the way we trained. For example, let's imagine there are two teams in a square where the sides measure 30 metres, and one of the teams is trying to hold onto the ball. If I reduce the sides of the square from 30 to 10 metres, I immediately change everything because I force the players closer together, which leads to more physical contact, more aggressiveness, more competitiveness, and so on. I also introduced another change – the compulsory use of shin-guards."

The Benfica team changed radically in only two months, as first choice players became dispensable, and dispensable players became first choice.

However, a situation arose immediately after the match against Boavista, which had left a lasting effect on the relationship between José Mourinho and the player, Maniche.

Aware that much needed to be changed, Mourinho decided to schedule a joint practice with Benfica's B team. He was still getting to know the club, and so he placed the B players on one side, and the seniors who hadn't played against Boavista on the other, together with a few others. As he had been sent off at Bessa Stadium, Maniche was one of the players to be called up. José Mourinho wanted this match to be as realistic as possible, and had therefore asked the referee to carry out his duties seriously. Everything was set up so that Mourinho could have a better understanding of the real potential of the B players.

A mere two minutes into the match, Maniche was responsible for a very hard tackle on an 'opponent'. The referee didn't have to think twice and immediately sent him off. Mourinho was watching from the top of the stands at Luz when he saw the player on his way to the changing rooms. He reached for his mobile phone at once, and told one of his assistants to order Maniche to run around the pitch until the end of the first half. The order was given and Maniche made a point of making it known that he was not happy about this – so much so, that eight minutes later he'd only done two laps, clearly showing his lack of interest in training. Mourinho told him to head for the showers.

We must have character; I only go to war with those I trust

When Maniche arrived for practice the next day, José Mourinho was waiting for him.

"It took you 8 minutes to run 800 metres yesterday. That means one of two things: you either have a problem on your mind that needs to be solved, or you have a physical problem, and you still need to find a solution for it. So, you're going to train with the B team, and when you feel that you no longer have a mental or physical problem, come and see me."

Maniche went to the B team, and at the end of the fourth day, he spoke to José Mourinho, apologising for his unprofessional attitude, and telling him that he had no problems at all. Mourinho placed him in Benfica's main team again, but made him pay a fine of 1,000 Euros.

A few weeks later, Maniche was Benfica's captain, and today he is one of the players who is vitally important to FC Porto's success. In the changing rooms, Mourinho is known as Maniche's 'godfather'.

The next game for Benfica was scheduled for Thursday, 28 September. It was a UEFA Cup match. Their opponents, the Swedish team Halmstads, playing at home, had beaten them 2-1 in the first leg. For José Mourinho it was his debut in European competition and one in which his team had to reverse a negative result. He was still looking for his first win as a coach. However, it was not to happen that night. Although he made some changes, they were not enough, and the final score was a 2-2 draw. Benfica were knocked out of the first round of the UEFA Cup. The next day, one of the headlines in the papers read: *"No ideas, no soul"*. Curiously enough, two characteristics that Mourinho did not lack.

Once again José Mourinho came to certain conclusions, and before the journalists in the press gallery at Luz Stadium he stated, *"We must have character, and those players who don't have it offer me no security in terms of moving ahead. I only go to war with those I trust."* A message and warning in one. Nevertheless, not everything had gone badly, and the Benfica coach even said that, *"the worst part was being eliminated, which is irreversible, but the team has improved in comparison to its past performances."*

> THE TURNING POINT

The next two league games were at Luz Stadium, against Sporting de Braga and Belenenses. Both Benfica and José Mourinho hankered after victory. The first match against Braga ended in a draw, and once more success was postponed. In the meantime, however, the team's tactical scheme was now quite different. Of the changes carried out by the coach, a completely new left wing stood out, with Rojas and Sabry having been replaced by 'the kids', Diogo Luís and Miguel. Paulo Madeira had also made way for Fernando Meira, who moved from the midfield to the defence axis, and Calado came in again to occupy Meira's former position. The first problems were soon to arise.

"The match against Braga was, perhaps, the turning point for the working group. At half-time we were losing and when I walked into the changing room, I saw Calado, none other than the captain, taking a shower. I couldn't believe it, but it was true. Calado told me he couldn't carry on playing. A few days before, a rumour had started that he was having a homosexual relationship with a Portuguese singer, and the Braga players had taken advantage of this and taunted him during the match. This affected him badly, and he was unable to play during the second half. Faced with this scenario, I substituted Calado and delivered an impassioned and emotional speech. There are times when a coach looks for a tactical change, and others where we shake things up on a psychological level. That's what I did. I went in search of their character and said something along the lines of, 'We don't have a captain, but

we'll go on as we are and we'll show all of them out there what we're made of.' The Benfica squad got the message of determination and courage, and went out and played a brilliant second half. They even went on to turn the score around from 0-1 to 2-1, and if there are matches where the final score is unfair, then this is one of them. At the very end, in the fourth minute of injury time, Braga managed a draw out of the blue, after a great second half where we dominated completely and where we could even have thrashed our opponents. That day was also set to mark the reconciliation between the fans and the team, despite the final draw, which is always a bad result for Benfica at Luz Stadium. At the end of the match, the team went onto the pitch to receive its members' ovation, as players and fans made up. All the factors involved in this game, and the way in which everything took place, resulted in a turning point in the mindset of the Benfica players. From there on, nothing was the same. 'My Benfica' began there and then."

According to Mourinho, it was a rejuvenated Benfica – more irreverent, more ambitious, and with greater solidarity – but essentially it was a team with a specific idea of the game. There was already a guiding principle on how to play, how to 'be' on the pitch and how to move. And so, it wasn't surprising when José Mourinho finally tasted his first victory at Benfica; his first win as head coach. It was against Belenenses and the 'reds' won 1-0. José Mourinho remained calm, and today he still maintains that the fact that it was the first win of his career didn't make him feel anything special.

> VILARINHO DEFEATS VALE E AZEVEDO

A few days later, there was a surprise in store for José Mourinho, which would have an effect on his future at Benfica. On 27 October 2000, against all expectations, João Vale e Azevedo lost the elections to Manuel Vilarinho. Vilarinho's statements during the run-up to the elections came to mind, but José Mourinho remained unshakable. The president is responsible for taking decisions, and the coach for training. That's what Mourinho did, and waited for Vilarinho to fulfil his promise to the Benfica fans, once more recalling one of the catch phrases of the election campaign: *"Toni is my coach."* But when the Benfica members voted, had they been thinking about a technical change, or had they simply been thinking about a change in the Board? It seemed the latter was more likely, and Manuel Vilarinho did not immediately dismiss José Mourinho. The recent results and the growing empathy between the coach and the members forced the new president to postpone this decision. Later, live on two Portuguese television channels, he stated that *"Toni will be coach, but Mourinho stays until the end of the season."* He was signing a 'non aggression pact', at least until further developments. Meantime, Mourinho knew his fate was sealed and that he was a sort of 'short-term' coach, as the Board prepared for the new season in a manner that would pave the way for Toni, Manuel Vilarinho's proclaimed coach. During this time, players were even signed without informing the Benfica coach. He had no knowledge of these acquisitions, which included players like Rui Baião, Ricardo Esteves, Roger and André. José Mourinho felt like 'cannon fodder' and nothing more. Even so, he continued at the helm of the 'red' ship.

Mourinho was perfectly aware that he was a sort of 'short-term' coach

"A touch of personal pride made me stay on at Benfica. I felt I couldn't leave without showing them I could do a good job. Today, I admit it was a mistake to stay. My insistence can be put down to my age and inexperience. I was a 'kid' who needed to prove his worth to the others, and that's why I stayed. I wouldn't do it again today. However, I don't think it was a waste of time. I proved something while I was there. Without having won anything, I conquered a place for myself by building a strong and united team that could take us somewhere. This also ate away at me, as I felt incredibly angry that I was raising a child I would have to abandon."

The match that followed the elections was played at the Benfica Stadium against Campomaiorense. Having gone a month without losing – something unheard of in the club's recent past – Benfica again won, 2-0, with João Tomás scoring both goals. José Mourinho remained true to his principles, and despite Benfica having a new president and his job being on the line, he praised someone he thought deserving. In a gesture of thanks, and without thinking about the consequences, Mourinho dedicated the win to João Vale e Azevedo.

He told the papers, *"I would like to dedicate this victory to the president who signed me and to wish the new president all the best for the future."*

However, the immediate future didn't hold much luck in store for Manuel Vilarinho. The next match would be in Madeira, against Marítimo. Benfica hadn't won at the Barreiros Stadium for the past five seasons. Cheered on by their good results, and accompanied by the new president, the team set off for the island on 3 November, with Manuel Vilarinho promising the papers he would *"bring them luck"*. The president's debut was a day to be forgotten and the match ended 3-0 in Marítimo's favour.

Mourinho promised to correct the defence, and Benfica started preparing to welcome Farense. Changes were made, and they returned to victory by beating the team from the Algarve 2-1.

It was during this week that a storm was brewing at the Luz Stadium. This time the crisis started in the changing rooms.

> THE SABRY CASE

The first real media problem that José Mourinho faced as Benfica coach involved the Egyptian, Sabry. From the very beginning, Mourinho had tried to discipline him on the field – to instil a certain measure of group culture in the player. However, in reality, there are attitudes or mindsets in our professional and social life that can't be changed within a reasonable space of time. Early on, José Mourinho had realised he could be facing one of these cases. A 'tug-of-war' had slowly been building up between coach and player. Now, suddenly, the rope snapped on Sabry's side. The player gave an interview to a sports paper, expressing his dissatisfaction with what was happening on the pitch. He complained about being placed on the left flank and having to follow strict tactical directions. He wanted to be directly behind the striker, free to move wherever he wished to. That's how he liked playing, and that's how he wanted to play. In this way, Sabry stood in direct opposition to the coach's philosophy.

José Mourinho acted swiftly, and now admits that he may have been a little too hard on the player.

"In hindsight, I think I was too hard on Sabry. I may even admit something

I wasn't aware of at the time, which is that Sabry ended up being somewhat of a victim of a situation that he hadn't entirely created himself. As I found out later, during the interview someone opposed to Vale e Azevedo was with him, and in some way led him to make those declarations. That same person also distorted some statements when translating for him. Sabry would reply using 4 or 5 words, and then the translation would run for 4 or 5 sentences, using 40 or 50 words. Thus, the interview wasn't entirely given by Sabry. I sometimes feel that the interview was given to cause problems for me, to see how I would handle the situation."

And José Mourinho handled the situation – in his own way. He remembered how he'd promised to be loyal to his players, 'face to face' – the exact opposite of what Sabry was doing by running off to the media to 'leave' messages for the coach and to express his dissatisfaction. Mourinho decided to adopt the player's rules and choice of weapons. Two days later, at a press conference at Luz Stadium, it was inevitable that questions would arise. No less inevitable was Mourinho's reply to Sabry.

Extremely methodical, José Mourinho has made a note of everything that he's done from the very beginning of his professional life. This began when he was still coaching juniors for Vitória de Setúbal. A little notebook is all he needs to set down everything he does and thinks in relation to his work.

He turned to his diary then to recall all the notes he'd taken down on Sabry.

"I turned to a whole set of truths that, as a rule, coaches keep to themselves. In this case, a player had been disloyal to me, and instead of

taking advantage of my open-door policy to speak to me, he'd chosen to speak to the press. So, I felt my answer should be public and convincing. I referred to how Sabry had often lost ball possession, in contrast to the few times he'd managed to regain the ball; and I also spoke of how I'd once waited eight minutes for him to enter play because he decided, among other things, to change his boots three times."

Thus, before the match against Farense, for which Sabry hadn't been selected, there were some interesting headlines in the papers, such as: *"Mourinho crushing. It's hard to like him"* or *"This is Benfica, not PAOK Salonica. I'm in charge here"*.

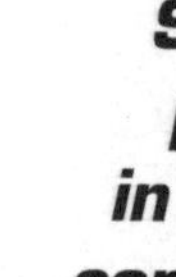

Support poured in from all corners, and from many people

And in the descriptions of the 'confrontation' between coach and player, Mourinho's reasoning won out. Sabry wanted to play as a number 10. Mourinho replied he had played that position against Belenenses, and that in 16 minutes the team from Belém had managed to counter-attack on five occasions due to balls lost by Sabry. According to Mourinho, *"a 'number 10 player' must display a high tactical level in order to be a link between the defence and attack, but not the defence and attack of the opponent."* Then, Sabry went on to complain that he'd played little in the last few matches. The coach had sent him on 28 minutes before the end of the match with Paços de Ferreira. Sabry had taken eight minutes to change his boots, and so was left with only 20 minutes to play. José Mourinho recalled, *"The players on the bench had raised their hands to their heads and sat dumbstruck, watching what was happening. In 28 minutes Sabry would have had more time to do what he hadn't managed to do in 20 minutes."* Mourinho also criticised the player for the absurd number of times he was offside, his lack of tactical awareness, and his failure to score.

> A SQUAD SPLIT DOWN THE MIDDLE

In the week following the match against Farense, another test of fire loomed. They were to play the always difficult Vitória de Guimarães, in the city known as Portugal's 'cradle' – the birthplace of the nation. Without knowing it, we were watching the beginning of the end of Mourinho's time at Benfica. Apart from all the difficulties they naturally expected, the team had to face yet another: to break the spell of bad luck, Benfica – almost at the end of the first half of the season – still hadn't managed to win an away match.

The Benfica party headed north to a hotel complex in Braga. There, José Mourinho was once again faced with an hilarious scene.

When they had arrived at the hotel, with no director from Benfica accompanying them, Mourinho was faced with a harsh reality: the team was divided between two separate buildings. It was the same hotel, but divided into two buildings. Half the team were on one side, together with all the directors who were to join them later, and 500 or 600 metres away, on the other side, were the other half. Someone had booked the rooms in a most unique and extraordinary way.

"When I arrived in Braga I realised that the rooms had been booked the following way: half of the team in one building, and the other half in another. One of the hotel buildings was better than the other, and there weren't enough rooms for everyone. The person responsible for the bookings had sacrificed team unity in favour of the comfort of the directors and their partners, and had unbelievably chosen to separate the players. I couldn't believe it, but the hotel showed me the faxes that had been sent from the Luz Stadium, proving that Benfica had booked the rooms this way. As there was no director with me, I had to solve this problem. I immediately told the hotel manager that we would only stay there if we could all stay together."

Faced with this absurd reality, José Mourinho didn't waver in his decision to have the whole squad in the same building. His insistence led to a change in the way the rooms were allocated. It was the directors and their partners who had to move.

The next day Benfica beat Vitória de Guimarães 4-0 at the Dom Afonso Henriques Stadium. Benfica were finally playing good football and the players increasingly believed in their abilities. Within the heart of the group, people began to talk of winning the league. Every day, the Benfica members expressed their total support for the coach. Yet despite all this progress, relations with the Board continued the way they'd been. Nothing had changed, and the rare meetings between the coach and the Board were cold and distant.

"It was clear to me that the Board's situation was becoming more and more difficult. The members were on my side, as were the players, and the results had started to appear. Support poured in – for my players and me – from all corners, and from many people.

I felt that there was this idea in the air that my desire to stay on at Benfica after the end of the season might come to something. I slowly began to believe that this was possible. At the time, I even had a lunch with Mozer and António Santos, where the latter said, 'If things continue this way, how will it be possible to change coach?'."

> LAST MATCH AS BENFICA'S COACH

The match with Sporting was coming up. Mourinho didn't yet know that it would be his last as Benfica coach.

In the week before the match, Portugal witnessed another great sporting event: the Masters tennis tournament was held in Lisbon. José Mourinho enjoys tennis a great deal, and he didn't want to miss the opportunity of seeing eight of the best players in the world.

"I was in the pavilion with Carlos Mozer, and when I looked round, I saw around 75% of the Sporting squad 'parading' around the Masters tournament. I immediately thought, 'These guys are here on the catwalk and I'm going to hammer them.' I thought they were overly confident. They were the champions, the stronger ones, and so there they were prancing around instead of thinking about that weekend's match. I told Mozer, "We're going to beat these guys. Tomorrow we'll use this situation to our advantage, and when we get to the practice we're going to poison our 'brood'. That's what I said, and that's what I did. When I got there I told them that the Sporting players had spent most of their time at the Masters tournament, obviously

thinking that they would thrash us by around six goals, and so on. I did what I'd set out to do, because I managed to get my players 'worked up', but today I must confess that I exaggerated. It's perfectly normal for someone to watch a tennis match and not lose sight of his objective. However, it's also normal for a coach to take advantage of this fact in order to build up team morale and to use the situation to achieve certain objectives. In one way or another, the Benfica players felt disdained by their opponents and that worked in our favour. They refused to be the 'underdogs'."

Apart from the psychological aspect, we also trained and rehearsed our tactics intensely. To beat Sporting, everything needed to be planned to a T and, if possible, we needed some surprises.

"There was a situation which was perhaps fundamental to our win. I remember that one of Sporting's weapons was César Prates' constant runs upfield. From the many videos I'd seen, I realised that César Prates had practically no defensive worries, because he was used to the opponent's left winger being a second left-sided defender who would keep up with his offensive incursions. Knowing this, I planned to make this situation work for us. But how? Instead of Miguel, our left-winger, keeping up with César Prates, I decided that our midfielders could do that. So, when the Sporting player

ran upfield, they'd 'swing' to the left and would keep up with and defend his incursions. This meant that Miguel would be free to run upfield and 'explore' the gap created when Sporting's right back moved forward. In this way Miguel caused many imbalances and, after a certain point in the match, César Prates stopped attacking. This then influenced the midfield itself, which also stopped 'swinging' to the left, thus creating a new imbalance in that part of the pitch. We inverted this situation on the other side with Sporting's defence. Carlitos would fall back, allowing Rui Jorge to surge forward. As the latter did so, he'd force André Cruz, a slower player, to double up his efforts on the right side. Thus, the Sporting players didn't cover a large part of the pitch, which was an opportunity for us to explore. These are some of the situations that lead me to conclude that tactically-speaking we prepared well for the match against Sporting."

If the match hadn't been against Sporting, I would have sent the players home

Despite having observed and prepared everything in relation to Benfica's opponents, another surprise lay in store for Mourinho – once again from inside the club itself. A week after the incident at the hotel in Braga, the coach had assumed that the 'hotel saga' was over. With the Benfica-Sporting match set for Saturday night, 3 December, the team had one last practice the day before, in the morning. They then had lunch and headed for a hotel in Lisbon, where they would spend the night. They usually stayed at the Meridien Hotel and José Mourinho, sitting upfront in the Benfica coach, was going over his notes of the week's practice. He didn't notice that they were headed elsewhere. He felt people moving in the seats behind him and realised they'd already come to a halt. When he looked around he saw that everything was different. He didn't recognise the hotel and had to read 'Hotel Altis' to know where he was. Thinking there was some kind of mistake, he turned to question the driver who'd dropped him off at the Meridien so often, *"Moreira, what's going on? Why are we here?"* He could scarcely believe the answer he was given. *"Mister, this is where I was told to come,"* said the Benfica driver, as he shrugged his shoulders. And that is how José Mourinho came to know that the Benfica directors had decided to change hotels.

"If the match had been against any team, other than Sporting, I would have sent the players home. That was my first reaction. So many thoughts went through my head. From sending the players home and telling them at what time to be at the Luz Stadium the next day, to my leaving at that very moment. But the match was against Sporting, and I knew all too well what the derby represented for all Benfica fans. I also couldn't do it because in case of defeat, my players would be left on their own. Imagine what they'd say about them, where had they been, etc. I took two deep breaths and got off the coach.

Later that day, Shéu Han explained to me that for economic reasons João Salgado had decided to change hotel. The question remained – why hadn't I been told? Shéu took full responsibility for what had happened, telling me he'd forgotten to inform me of the Board's decision."

But José Mourinho was fed up with so many 'mistakes' and didn't accept his apology. Instead he thought, *"They're provoking me again."*

With all this taking place amidst players and journalists, time moved on towards the match. José Mourinho remembers driving to the Luz Stadium that day. Tensions were running high, both because they were playing Sporting, and because of all the previous events. Mourinho let none of this show as he rode upfront in the coach, looking distractedly at the streets they were leaving behind. Then suddenly everything changed.

"The turning point was the Hotel Penta. From there on, I could no longer be absent. There was movement all around, flags appeared, and shouts of encouragement were getting louder and louder. It was as if we were already at the match. We couldn't think of anything else."

Now all that was left to do, was to play. There was nothing else to be done. With José Mourinho, every player knows five days before a match which team will be playing from the start. In the practices throughout the week, they also get to understand how they will play and which tactics will be used for the opponents in question. Given the way work had progressed, José Mourinho felt that the team was motivated and consistent. He still remembers the remarkable way João Tomás recovered from a knee sprain, and was fit to take on Sporting when everyone had thought that this would be impossible. Everything was in place for a win over their long-standing rivals, and nothing led Mourinho to believe that this would be his last match as Benfica's coach.

"I was only thinking about the football and I wanted this match to be a landmark. It would be our fourth consecutive win, we'd beat our great rivals – who were none other than the National Champions – we'd reduce the distance between us and first place, and it would raise morale among the 'troops'. Essentially, it was about re-launching the team into the league."

As usual, Mourinho didn't make a long speech in the changing rooms before the match. He waited for the players to make their way to the pitch for the first warm-up, and then he headed there, too. There were already an impressive number of fans, and the colour red stood out above any other. On the pitch, he turned around and admired the grand stadium. Seen from down below, and bursting with people, it looks even more impressive – and more overwhelming. There, too, José Mourinho could feel the confidence and hope, the Benfica morale. More than ever in their recent past, the Benfica fans had begun to believe again. The atmosphere was set for victory – a draw, which normally wouldn't have been a bad result, was no longer enough. José Mourinho then watched the players warming up. He saw the enthusiasm and confidence they radiated and, perhaps for the first time since he'd become the Benfica coach, he had only one option: to win.

Benfica got off to a good start. Maniche could have scored in the first minute as he went one-on-one with the Sporting goalkeeper, Nelson. *"It didn't start off badly, but it could have been better – if it had been a goal,"* thought Mourinho. In any case, the dice had been thrown and orders were being followed. The Benfica coach had asked the players to take the initiative right from the beginning. He wanted them to attack when they had the ball, and he called for offensive pressing when the opponents had the ball. This philosophy immediately led to the first goal opportunity for Maniche – many others would follow.

"The first goal was from a penalty in the first half. Some trainers prefer not to watch, but not me. I always watch the penalty being taken. This time, however, the referee asked for it to be repeated because a player of ours had entered the penalty area before the penalty shot. Fortunately, Van Hooijdonk scored again and brought the score to 1-0. At half-time I was told that Sporting were going to make a substitution. They were playing with Acosta, a striker, and I was told that Spear would go on. That meant they'd start the second half with two forwards in my area, where I only had two defenders, Marchena and Meira.

At half-time I spoke to the players about the substitution that Augusto Inácio, the Sporting coach, would make. I wanted to test their 'mettle', and I asked Marchena and Meira if they had any fears about playing two against two, knowing they could make no mistakes or be afraid of the Sporting forwards. If they said "yes", I'd have to put Geraldo on, and defend three against two, with one defender left for support at the back. We'd probably manage to hold onto the game, but we'd hand over the initiative to our opponents. If they said "no", we'd keep to the same system and we'd have an advantage in the midfield, because for Spear to come on, a Sporting midfielder would have to go off. I was happy when Meira and Marchena didn't hesitate, and immediately gave me a sign: two against two! It's what I'd wanted to hear. I continued with Calado, Chano and Maniche in the midfield, against two Sporting players. I asked my midfielders to pass the ball to each other, thereby forcing the Sporting midfielders to run, and told them that when they were sure they could, they should launch quick counter-attacks. I also told them that I would make two substitutions after 10 minutes. Poborsky and João Tomás, two extremely fast forwards, would go on and substitute Rui Jorge and André Cruz. It was around then that we scored two goals in the second half."

João Tomás had barely gone on when he scored the second goal. It was then that José Mourinho did something that many Sporting fans have still not forgiven him for. In the heat of the moment, he made a fist and flexed his arm twice. Mourinho says it was an instinctive gesture – like any other he could have made. He didn't realise it could be so badly interpreted – as indeed it was. But he did it without any malice. It was a straight-forward gesture.

"I clearly remember that I did not celebrate the first goal. When the second goal came, it felt as if I'd won the game at that very moment. I thought "It's in the bag; we've won" and I made that gesture. After the third goal, I looked at the new third tier of stands and gave them a thumbs-up, because I felt the Benfica fans hadn't been this happy in recent times. Then, I still had time to send on Geraldo, which meant the debut of another player from the B team. I finished the game sitting calmly on the bench and savouring the moment."

When Jorge Coroado signalled the end of the match, José Mourinho immediately sought refuge in the changing rooms at Luz Stadium. He got up from the bench and, without giving the radio reporters on the pitch a chance, he hurried towards the stairs that lead to the changing rooms. At the bottom of the stairs he turned left and, while the Benfica footballers were still celebrating on the pitch, he set off on his own down the corridor that leads to the players' and coaches' changing rooms. Once in his office, he sat down at his desk and looked at the photograph of his wife and kids, feeling he had fulfilled his duty. For a few minutes he felt a strange inner peace, as if nothing else mattered apart from his family. But things weren't quite like that.

"Suddenly a whirl of ideas and feelings bubbled up inside me. The hotel 'switch' nobody had told me about came to mind again, as did the hotel mix-up in Braga, the players they'd signed without my knowledge, the dismissal promises they'd made, and so on. Now I wanted to see how they would get out of this scrape."

Mourinho had gone back in time, and while he was 'rewinding' he realised he'd been a puppet in the hands of the new Board. He'd gone from Vale e Azevedo's trump card to one of Manuel Vilarinho's disposable cards. He was sure that all it would take was two consecutive losses for this to happen. And then he savoured the moment once more. Beating Sporting 3-0 would make the fans deliriously happy, and Benfica were in a position to fight for first place in the league. But what about the Board? What were the Benfica directors thinking? Were they satisfied? Or not? And what would things be like now? José Mourinho was no longer certain of anything. He remembered yet another event that had taken place that very week, before the match against Sporting.

José Mourinho had heard of a conversation between a Benfica director and another from Sporting. At a certain point, the Benfica director had come out with this 'gem': *"Let's see if you guys can come here and win, so that we can send that guy packing."* Both directors are still working for the respective clubs, and for that reason José Mourinho doesn't want to reveal their names.

Mourinho realised that he had been a puppet in the hands of the board

The noisy celebrations abruptly interrupted Mourinho's thoughts. The squad had begun to arrive back in the changing rooms and their happiness could not be contained. Despite the hurt he felt at being unfairly treated, even though he'd been doing excellent work, José Mourinho felt compelled to hug his players and to thank them. Without winning any titles, Benfica had managed, with a lot of work and perseverance, to overcome their shortcomings in just two months. They once again respected and admired themselves, and most importantly, they believed in the near future. The giant had awoken, and once awake it is very difficult to take on.

> IT'S ALL OR NOTHING

After a short celebration with the squad, Mourinho returned to his office. He undressed, then before stepping into the shower, he called Tami. Sitting in his underwear, with his feet on the table, he relived it all with his family. That's when he became the lead in a scene he would later regret.

"I was on the phone with my wife when Manuel Vilarinho appeared at my door. The Benfica president stood in the doorway, waiting for me to tell him to come in. I ignored him completely. I simply continued speaking to Tami until he tired of waiting and left. I don't know what he wanted or what he had to tell me. I only know that I regret my reaction, but I can't go back to make it right. I've already had the opportunity to apologise to him for what happened and, here and now, I apologise once more."

At that point, it was as if José Mourinho was a wary animal and his reactions were unpredictable.

The director of Benfica's Communications Office appeared after Manuel Vilarinho. João Malheiro asked him to go to the press gallery for the usual post-match interview, the short interview that trainers have to do for television as soon as the match is over. José Mourinho didn't want to go, and agreed to pay the respective fine. He showered and quickly left the Luz Stadium. Half an hour after the end of the game, he was in his car, stuck in traffic. The radio was on and he still caught some of the comments about the game made by Sporting's coach, Augusto Inácio, and some Benfica players.

He then had to divide his attention between what the radio was saying and the attention coming from astonished Benfica fans, as they realised that there was the Benfica coach who, only thirty minutes before, had beaten their neighbour and rival, Sporting. One thing he heard, and would remember for a long time, came from a Benfica fan who, filled with enthusiasm, shouted out, *"With you in Benfica, we'll still win everything this season. Go for it, Mourinho!"* The irony was not lost on José Mourinho. *"Strange. While some encourage me, others try to discourage me. Is this really what Benfica's grandness is all about? In order to coach Benfica, will I have to deal with this strange paradox where some support me and others reject me?"*

He started to have doubts about the immediate future. Should he continue with Benfica, or not? Should he sort out his future with the club's Board once and for all? Should he wait to be sacked? Should he simply close this door?

It was overcast. The rain that had fallen during most of the match had now given way to strong winds. José Mourinho was on the Bridge *25 de Abril*, on his way home to Setúbal, when a powerful gust of wind shook his car. He held the steering wheel tightly and changed lanes, feeling safer on the inside lane, even if the violent wind was to return. He carried on home, the shelter from the storm – from all the storms.

But José Mourinho couldn't stop thinking about Benfica. He was proud about how they'd made a comeback at the most difficult time in the season. He couldn't contain his satisfaction as he remembered that against opponents such as Boavista, Marítimo, Belenenses, Guimarães and Sporting, he had managed to perform the 'miracle' of restoring Benfica to… Benfica.

They've had time to see whether or not they like my work

In theory, an easier period was on its way. Benfica would now be entering a cycle where their adversaries would be Alverca, Gil Vicente, Desportivo das Aves and Estrela da Amadora. In terms of the immediate future, José Mourinho had every right to think that, with some luck and a lot of hard work, they could make it to the top of the League by Christmas.

On his way home, on the motorway linking Lisbon to Setúbal, Mourinho took a decision that would shake up the sporting nation throughout Portugal.

"It's all or nothing now. I love my work and I want to stay in this club, so they either want me to stay on and offer me the working conditions I need, or they want none of this and I'll leave. After a 3-0 win over Sporting, it's time for the Board to commit itself. They've had time to see whether or not they like my work; whether they think it's good or not. This is my only chance to know if it's possible for me to continue here or if I'm merely paving the way for a successor. Yes, it is! Me and them, we all have to take decisions now!"

Deep down, no matter how contradictory it might have seemed, José

Mourinho was convinced that the Board wouldn't let him down. The growing empathy with the club members, a united squad, where the overwhelming majority of the players supported him, and the fantastic results the team had achieved were, he thought, sufficient reasons to keep him on. Furthermore, the more strength the Board gives a coach, the stronger a football coach is. José Mourinho wanted the players to know that he wasn't in Benfica for the short-term. The future was thus a challenge. Given time, how far could he take Benfica? His mind was once again flooded with ideas, and all his desires centred on the future of Benfica. He had no more doubts. The club's Board had to decide, and it had to do so in his favour. José Mourinho was all too well aware of a certain clause in his contract. If Vale e Azevedo had won the elections, then the six-month contract would have automatically been renewed for a further two years. Vale hadn't won, but Vilarinho could still renew it.

After a good night's sleep, the Benfica coach wasted no time, phoning Manuel Vilarinho first thing in the morning. After sleeping on it, and talking to Tami, José Mourinho had decided to 'tone down' his aspirations. He would ask Manuel Vilarinho for only another year's contract. He also decided to bluff. He thought that putting a little pressure on the president might help, and so he would say that another club was interested in his services.

Manuel Vilarinho, possibly smarting from the coach's attitude the night before, or for some other reason, didn't take José Mourinho's call. Determined to resolve the matter as quickly as possible, the coach phoned João Malheiro, who took the call. And so it was that José Mourinho spoke of his intentions to Benfica's Director of Communications. *"João, a club has made me an offer, and if Benfica doesn't renew my contract for another year, I'm leaving. I'm not even asking for more money. I'll stay on the same salary I'm getting now, but I want another year. Please convey what I've told you to the president."* Although they weren't great friends, there was a certain level of familiarity that allowed João Malheiro to say somewhat disapprovingly, *"Hey man, you're mad. Don't do it. What do you think you're doing?"* But José Mourinho wouldn't back down; nothing would sway him. *"As I said, you either want me to stay on or you don't. The decision must be taken now. Talk to the president and then let me know something."* With no other alternative, João Malheiro was forced to pass on the message to Manuel Vilarinho. The Benfica president replied, saying that he would see Mourinho the next day.

Two days after the match with Sporting, the clouds had lifted and although it was cold, the rain had given way to sun. Through his bedroom window, José Mourinho felt immediately cheered by the sight of the sun framed in a clear, blue sky. The Sado River was calm and shining, reflecting the sun's rays that bathe it every morning at eight. Everything was off to a perfect start.

During the trip to Lisbon he tried not to think about the decisive meeting he was about to have. When he arrived at the Stadium, he went straight to the changing rooms where the players were getting ready for the first practice of the week. Not forgetting the pledge of loyalty he'd made to them from the start, José Mourinho informed the squad about the meeting he was about to have, and Carlos Mozer led the practice that day, with all of them aware of what was happening.

Manuel Vilarinho saw José Mourinho in the Stadium's presidential office. The president already knew what was to be discussed, so no preamble was necessary. With president and coach sitting face to face, the meeting was dominated by pragmatism. Vilarinho went straight to the matter in hand. *"As far as I'm concerned, yes! You can stay on for another year. I know what's being done on a football level in this club, and I'm pleased. I'd give you another year's contract, but my Board doesn't want to, and neither do the investors."*

It was clear to José Mourinho that the president's hands were tied, and that his will alone wouldn't be enough to keep him on as coach. There were other interests at work in the catacombs at Luz, and those interests did not include José Mourinho. They were aimed at someone else, at least with regard to the first team coach. Manuel Vilarinho tried to sway Mourinho and asked him to stay, suggesting that maybe towards the end of the season, after a job well done, things might change and that he might be in a better position in terms of a more permanent post. Not for one moment was José Mourinho tempted by Manuel Vilarinho's words. As a result of all that had happened in recent times, he was much too wary to believe in anything that anyone on the Board had to say. Now, it was either down in 'black and white', or it was nothing. And nothing it was! It was agreed there and then that Mourinho would leave Benfica immediately – he wouldn't even carry out another practice. There was only time to settle accounts and bid farewell to the many friends that he still has at Luz today.

The news spread quickly. A press conference was called at the Luz Stadium, and the fans started to gather at the entrance. It was then that José Mourinho witnessed one of the scenes that most disgusted him in the whole process of leaving Benfica.

The president's hands were tied

A few minutes after leaving Manuel Vilarinho's office, Mourinho went to the toilet. He walked in and overheard a conversation that one of the Benfica vice-presidents was having on his mobile phone with a journalist. The sinister individual, who is still on the Board today, said, *"You can write that the guy asked us to triple his salary to renew the contract. He only wants money, and we would never give in to such blackmail."*

This was a conversation Mourinho himself heard; he was not told about it by someone else, and faced with such a hideous lie, you can well imagine what was going through his mind. Nevertheless, he kept calm – apparently and impressively calm. There were more important things for him to take care of.

Today, time has softened the conflict.

"I admit that I used blackmail on Manuel Vilarinho. Telling him that 'either you give me a year's contract or I'll leave because another club is interested in me' is a form of blackmail. However, truth be told, this blackmail wasn't accepted – not as a matter of principle, but because Manuel Vilarinho couldn't accept it. If he could have, he would have given into the blackmail because – and I'm sure of this today – that was what he wanted.

On the other hand, I am still a little upset about the way in which I treated Manuel Vilarinho. Today I would never have told journalists that 'Vilarinho has no say over anything.' I am convinced that Manuel Vilarinho is a good man, who didn't deserve the way I treated him. It was wrong and unfair of me to have made certain accusations against him."

>> CHAPTER III **THE TRANSITION**

LEIRIA 2001/02

LUÍS DUQUE SPEAKS
MEETING UP WITH PINTO DA COSTA AGAIN
THE MOVE TO UNIÃO DE LEIRIA
MANUEL JOSÉ, THE JUNGLE AND TARZAN
THE DOUBTS OF JOÃO BARTOLOMEU
CHAMPION WITH 4 PLAYERS FROM LEIRIA
BENFICA ONCE AGAIN
LUÍS FILIPE VIEIRA STEPS UP THE PRESSURE

>> CHAPTER III **THE TRANSITION**

With Benfica behind him, rumours circulated almost simultaneously that Sporting were interested in signing Mourinho. In fact, it was a story that the Benfica Board had put out. José Mourinho's bluff had boomeranged on him.

By pure coincidence, Augusto Inácio had also left the club from Alvalade after the match they'd played at the Luz Stadium. In some way, though for different reasons, the match between the two rivals ended up being directly linked to the departure of both coaches, which led to a situation that had never happened before in the history of the two clubs.

Just as with Benfica, over at Alvalade, the mood was also far from perfect. The champions, Sporting, were not producing the desired results, and to lose 3-0 to Benfica was the worst result of all. Humiliation hung over the Stadium of the Lion. [7]

> *LUÍS DUQUE SPEAKS*

Luís Duque was the strong man at Sporting Clube de Portugal, and was regarded as one of the key people responsible for their having won the league the year before. So, he was living in a state of grace. He tells us what was going on in Alvalade at that time.

"We had a significantly better squad, in order to respond to the demands imposed by the three 'fronts' the team was involved in. However, Sporting didn't manage to play with the regularity and effectiveness we had hoped for, in a year where SAD [8] itself had set its sights very high. As high as the Club's titles.

There were clearly several main causes for the team's weak performances in the second half of matches, and therefore for the results: the changes put forward by the coach in terms of fitness training; inadequate programming

7. *The lion is the symbol of Sporting Clube de Portugal.*
8. *SAD; Sociedad Anónima Desportiva – a public limited company (football club).*

during the pre-season, which had been mainly aimed at players who weren't going to play, whilst those who should have played didn't – and, as I recall, the fact that nine international players were late arriving back from the European Championship.

A certain amount of unease arose, and so began the traditional 'witch-hunt' to track down those responsible for the current state of affairs: directors, coaches, players, referees, etc.

Players who'd left and were needed; players who'd joined us and weren't needed at all; doctors, trainers, directors and assessors who should never have left: all of these were pretexts for the usual 'opinion makers' – commentators, distinguished personalities, ex-, current, and aspirant directors – to give SAD a good thrashing, whom they could not forgive for the supreme affront of having won the league 18 years later, and whom they wanted to spite as they had not been the 'chosen ones'.

But no one was interested in the real reason, the only cause that could be scientifically proved. It wouldn't make the front pages or get you photographs in the papers.

And it was in this state of turmoil and anguish that the team lost at Luz to its old rival, and by 3-0 as well. It was 3 December, and we'd be playing Belenenses in the next game in a high-risk match, with our confidence completely shaken. Something had to be done. There was still time."

Luís Duque began to look across the road and remembered José Mourinho

At this point – not even a day after Mourinho's departure from Benfica – the agent, José Veiga, with whom Mourinho had a special professional relationship, called him. Veiga wanted to know if he was interested in coaching Atlético de Madrid, a Spanish club in the First Division that wasn't performing very well. In Spain, the law states that a coach can only work there if he has held the same post in his country of origin for at least two years. This meant that for Mourinho to go to Spain, he needed to have coached a First Division club in Portugal for at least two years. Neither José Mourinho, nor José Veiga, were fully aware of this prerequisite, which Mourinho clearly did not meet. Through Angel Vilda, Benfica's Spanish assistant coach since the time of Jupp Heynckes, they got in touch with the coaches' union in Spain. Now clearly aware of the requirements, they set aside the Atlético de Madrid possibility.

It was then that Sporting was first mentioned, some time after José Mourinho had left Benfica.

Veiga was once again the middle-man. *"Sporting doesn't have a head coach. They like the game philosophy you've shown as a coach. Luís Duque has a lot of admiration for you and he would like to meet you."*

With nothing to lose and, most likely, nothing to gain, José Mourinho accepted the invitation.

In the meantime, 'something was being done' in Alvalade and the Sporting directors had decided to change coach. Luís Duque began to look across the road [9] and remembered José Mourinho, while at the same time trying to resolve the situation with Augusto Inácio in the best and most dignified manner possible. Luís Duque again explains,

"In seeking a dignified solution suited to his status as a champion, we offered the head coach, Augusto Inácio, to whom Sporting will always owe a great deal for all he did for the Club, another post, whereby he'd maintain the same perks and benefits.

Meanwhile, in relation to José Mourinho, I must confess that as soon as I heard about Benfica's decision regarding his contract, I thought it was very strange and unexpected.

I knew of his past achievements, and I also knew that in Barcelona he sometimes led the first team, and that he was also responsible for their good results.

An assistant coach who'd coached Barcelona, and who displayed the character, knowledge and ambition that he did, had all the requirements to be successful. It was a question of time and opportunity. Was this big-time entry premature? It obviously wasn't.

In nine games, there were two draws, five wins and two defeats. The first defeat was in the very first game against Boavista, and the other in the match against Marítimo, where he risked everything and never gave in, despite losing unfairly as it was Benfica who'd given a brilliant performance that night. Next came Guimarães and another wonderful performance with a convincing 4-0 win, and then Sporting.

9. *The stadiums of Sporting and Benfica are on opposite sides of one of Lisbon's busiest roads.*

What impressed me most about José Mourinho was his capacity to mould a young team in his image – an aggressive, motivated, and winning team – with the available 'raw material', i.e. human material, and make any player believe that he was the best in the world in his position, when perhaps he wasn't.

As I later confirmed in conversations between the two of us, charisma, leadership, and a great deal of work and study were, and still are, the main qualities and ingredients of his success.

As I knew of the difficult relationship Mourinho had with the Board of his club, where he was considered as a short-term option and systematically shown little consideration – take for example the Braga and Lisbon hotel incidents – I asked a friend to convey my interest in counting on him in Sporting, if he decided to leave Benfica. All of this, trying to steer him away from entering into a commitment to anyone else, like Atlético de Madrid for example, as there was already talk that they were interested in signing him.

As is well-known, that Sporting-Benfica match spelt the departure of both coaches from their respective clubs, but for different reasons."

Following the conversation with José Veiga, Mourinho and the Sporting director had lunch together. They spoke of the future Alcochete Academy (Sporting's Training Centre), of the plans and projects for training Sporting players, the new stadium, ideas for the club's future, the Sporting squad – all in all, they spoke about Sporting's future. Essentially, it was a first encounter that enabled Luís Duque to get a more detailed understanding of Mourinho's ideas, in case he should decide to go ahead and sign the young coach. And that's where the contacts between Mourinho and Sporting directors ended.

Luís Duque himself would leave the club following this whole process; indeed he couldn't resist the 'Mourinho possibility'.

"When, two days later, I announced the departure of the Sporting coach at a press conference, José Mourinho had already announced that he too was leaving Benfica. Thus, faced with the hostile reaction of its members, Benfica – in an anticipatory gesture and amid a show of crocodile tears – cleverly, but also hypocritically, decided to blame Sporting's SAD for his departure, thereby trying to create problems for us in order to solve its own.

And at the time, it was painfully obvious that they didn't like Mourinho or his style.

Unfortunately for us, there was no time for negotiation. Everything happened quickly, in the worst of ways.

The negative reaction of some Sporting members at the press conference; Beto declaring that 'it could only be a sick joke'; the declarations by the Sporting president who, caught unprepared abroad, said, 'he's got nothing to recommend him' – all of this added together made it impossible to sign him.

It was the president of Sporting who said he didn't want me to be the club's coach

And I reiterate that the president was unprepared, because he was always extremely careful to support SAD's decisions, even those considered to be more controversial.

Immediately there was a shower of criticism from the 'usual distinguished personalities', to the delight of the media.

In the meantime, Sporting were preparing to place the first team in the hands of the 'historic' Fernando Mendes provisionally, while an agreement was ironed out with José Mourinho.

Ribeiro Teles suspended the contacts he'd been having with Victor Fernandez, as both he and the whole Board were pleased with the Mourinho possibility.

Sadly, it wasn't possible.

Personally, I lost the 'room for manoeuvre' and the authority necessary to carry out my work, and I learnt not to get involved in risky and draining projects without a basic 'network'.

Sporting lost the opportunity to have a coach who would have completely fitted in with their training project – an ambitious coach whose success was founded on his leadership abilities and on hard work, and who – with no offence meant to the 'old school' – opened the door to a new era in training methodology in Portugal.

A coach up to the challenge of demanding football in the 21st century."

Meanwhile, Manuel Fernandes had been chosen as Augusto Inácio's successor. José Mourinho, a long-time friend of the new Sporting coach, phoned him at once to congratulate him, and to distance himself from anything that might connect him to the Alvalade club.

As for what had happened backstage at Alvalade, José Mourinho drew his own conclusions.

"I think Luís Duque put my name forward. This was met with some contestation and he, as the 'champion leader', didn't accept their having vetoed my name. First it was the members, and then the Sporting president, Dias da Cunha, said he didn't want me to be Sporting's coach. And Luís Duque didn't accept this. He probably felt that his decision-making power had been undermined, which led him to resign. Basically, he was a victim of his admiration for me. It may not be a good comparison, but it was the same thing as having a president tell me to take that player off and put another one on. If that happened to me, I would leave. That's what Luís Duque did."

> MEETING UP WITH PINTO DA COSTA AGAIN

Around that time, Portugal played Holland at the Antas Stadium [10] in a qualifying match for the World Cup 2002. Mourinho returned to a home he'd known well during the two years as Bobby Robson's assistant coach, before they'd headed for Barcelona. He also met up with Porto president, Jorge Nuno Pinto da Costa, after not having seen each other for a rather long time. Life had taken them on separate paths, but their friendship remained. When they ran into each other again, Pinto da Costa was as happy as ever to see him.

"The relationship we'd always shared, which had become even stronger when I worked at Antas with Robson, hadn't been the slightest bit tarnished by my time at Benfica. The president was very happy to see me once again. We hugged, made some small chat and then Pinto da Costa left me in no doubt that one day I would be FC Porto's coach. He made sure I knew, however, that I wouldn't be the next one. He said, 'Do you know who's asked me for information about you? Alverca and Leiria.' Basically, in other words he was saying, 'If you are in any way waiting for Porto, you'd better look elsewhere because you won't be the next coach. There are some smaller clubs interested

10. *Antas Stadium: former name of FC Porto's Stadium.*

in you, so choose well and work even better. However, don't despair because your time at this Club will come. I know your worth and I like your work.' And this governed my actions, because I clearly understood the message."

José Mourinho was now convinced that he would coach FC Porto one day; he just didn't know when.

If he'd already decided that going to battle was the only path to take, he was now more certain than ever – even though he knew that things wouldn't be easy for him in the near future. 2001 had just begun, Christmas had passed and Mourinho had no coaching prospects in the near future. Even so, he wasn't flustered.

Pinto da Costa left me in no doubt that one day I would be FC Porto's coach

"Some Portuguese coaches prefer to work abroad, even if it's for a 'third-world' football club, or not to coach at all, rather than work for small teams in Portugal. That's not the case with me, nor will it ever be. The important thing is to work with dignity, and so I knew that I would have to go to battle and that, in the immediate future, I'd have to work with a small team. I was available to coach any team in the First Division, even if it was doomed for the 'drop'. However, I also knew that it would be difficult to find a job in a season already underway."

And that's what happened. Mourinho was unemployed. Once again he took advantage of this time to study and to relax with his family.

> *THE MOVE TO UNIÃO DE LEIRIA*

It was mid April, and José Mourinho was already tired of watching others play, when he was first contacted by a company called Media Capital, a shareholder in União de Leiria/SAD. Mourinho was asked to be present at a meeting; they wanted to assess his receptiveness to being the next coach at União de Leiria.

Once everybody had sat down at the meeting, Mourinho's first question was quick and direct. *"As União de Leiria is enjoying an excellent championship, why are you looking for a coach? At this moment you're in 7th place (*they would finish the season in 5th) *and you want me to do better?"*

José Mourinho knew it was almost impossible to do better and that the directors of União de Leiria should have been extremely pleased with what a club their size had managed to achieve so far. Ambition must always be present, but sometimes one must be careful not to want too much and risk losing everything.

José Mourinho felt he needed to understand what the club's directors were looking for. He was sure that better results weren't the reason for considering changing coach. And they weren't.

They explained that they'd been given a profile for a coach for the next season, and José Mourinho fitted that profile to a T. As for the current coach, Manuel José, the club was happy with the team's performance, but his profile didn't fit in with what União de Leiria wanted for the future.

Manuel José's departure from Leiria at the end of the season was therefore presented as being irreversible. They also went on to say that another two coaches were being contacted and evaluated. They all had a degree in Physical Education; both were focused on training, and were young and ambitious. José Mourinho was asked to study the possibility of taking charge of União de Leiria for the next season, and they emphasised the need for complete secrecy about the meeting.

Mourinho replied that both parties would have to study the situation more carefully. He would therefore draw up a report to present at the next meeting, where he would set out his plans for what could become his work at Leiria. Until then, they were to think about what would be best for all concerned.

The document setting out his direction was ready a couple of days later, and was handed in and analysed. Without great delay, José Mourinho was informed that the directors of União de Leiria had chosen him. From there on, they'd need to know if he'd accept the job, and if so they'd have to work out contract-related issues. Mourinho immediately said yes, and now the ball was in the president's court. All negotiations regarding the signing José Mourinho would be carried out by João Bartolomeu. It was also easy to come to an agreement on this point, and the coach accepted a salary of exactly half the amount he'd been making at Benfica – money was a consequence and not the objective.

Once more full of confidence in his abilities, José Mourinho asked João Bartolomeu for a single clause: that he could leave at the end of the season for one of the three big clubs – Benfica, Porto or Sporting – provided that he notified União de Leiria of such a decision a month before the end of the league.

From that moment on, having signed a contract, José Mourinho started quietly working towards the next season. The main objective was to do a good job in the First Division, and so there was no time to waste. He went up and down the country watching second division games, spent a month in Brazil, and watched hundreds of videos looking for players that might be of interest to União de Leiria.

> *MANUEL JOSÉ, THE JUNGLE AND TARZAN*

Mourinho calmly prepared União de Leiria's future. Then one day, one of the strangest incidents of his professional life took place. He was watching a sports programme on television and realised that Manuel José, the Leiria trainer at the time, was to be interviewed. He paid closer attention, but there was no way he could have expected what was to happen. He suddenly found himself embroiled in an absurd controversy. Manuel José stated, *"If Mourinho thinks this is a jungle, and that he is Tarzan, then he is greatly mistaken."* Manuel José then launched into a long tirade, full with strange comments and ideas. Mourinho realised that this attack on his ethics was happening because Manuel José hadn't received a phone call saying that he, José Mourinho, would be taking over as Leiria's next coach. Mourinho then found himself digging into his own memories and finding examples closer to home.

Mourinho was surprised by the aggressive attitude of his colleague Manuel José

"I am the son of a coach, and I watched my father coach many different clubs all over Portugal. I can never forget the most painful days for a football coach. It isn't a new idea, and it's been used time and time again through the decades: the psychological whipping. I saw my father being sacked several times, too many times. I never knew of anyone who would first phone him to give him some sort of justification. I had been through a similar situation myself just a few months before at Benfica. I got no phone call from the coach who succeeded me, but our friendship didn't end there and I continued thinking he was a fantastic person."

José Mourinho was surprised by the aggressive attitude of his colleague,

Manuel José, but alone at home he took advantage of the moment, which he considered funny, to laugh out loud. He thought to himself, *"What a fine and strange expression just right for the person speaking."* It was already late at night and José Mourinho went to bed with a clear conscience, knowing he had done nothing to lead to Manuel José being dismissed. The directors of União de Leiria had presented him with a *fait accompli*, so that even if it hadn't been him, someone else would have replaced the Leiria coach. Mourinho accepted the offer, he didn't regret it, and would do it all over again today.

It was also around this time that José Mourinho changed the assistant coach. Carlos Mozer had done an excellent job when he had worked with him at Benfica, and fully satisfied with his performance, he once again asked Mozer to join him on this new adventure. However, there was less money at Leiria and just like Mourinho, Mozer would also have to earn half of what he had been making previously. In the end, Carlos Mozer didn't accept the offer, for reasons that Mourinho perfectly understood. His whole personal life was centred in and around Lisbon, as were his business interests. The proposed salary wouldn't justify such a radical change in his life. However, they agreed to leave the door open to work together again some time in the future, either in the short- or the long-term.

Needing to sort out the assistant coach situation, José Mourinho started thinking of people who could replace Mozer. Once again Tami's help was to prove essential. Mourinho was sitting at home with a pen and paper as he thought of different possibilities, when his wife asked, *"What exactly are you thinking? Do you need someone who knows about training methodology, or someone who'll offer protection and friendship and has some experience with players?"*

José Mourinho's ideas weren't fixed, and so an answer came easily.

"I don't need someone who knows about methodology because that is my forté, not to mention the fact that I'm headstrong. No one can influence me in that regard. I want someone in the football world who knows how to speak to players, and who can assert himself and has authority in the changing rooms, and someone who is… big!" Both laughed at this last requirement, and then Tami said, *"So speak to Brito, he may be the person you're looking for."*

Baltemar Brito is a longstanding friend of the Mourinho family. Tall and lanky, he arrived from Brazil over twenty years ago. A centre back, he always played with his socks around his ankles and was one of the pillars of the famous Rio Ave of the '80s, which made it to the Portuguese Cup final, and was fifth in the First Division. The coach at the time was Mourinho Félix, father of José Mourinho who, in turn, also played for the club from Vila do Conde.

Brito struck up a friendship, not only with the father, but also with the son, and he went on to be a player who always accompanied Mourinho Félix. He was a player who could be trusted both on and off the pitch, and it was off the pitch that he got to know Tami, who at that time was already Mourinho's girlfriend. Many years later, when Tami brought his name up again, José Mourinho didn't think twice and immediately accepted his wife's suggestion. Today, every time he speaks of her, Brito affectionately calls her his 'godmother'.

As for Rui Faria, a Physical Education graduate like Mourinho, things had been arranged some time before. Rui Faria had done his training in Barcelona, and that's where the two had met. After a few conversations, it was clear that both had a similar approach to coaching and fitness training. From the beginning, Mourinho had realised that one day Rui Faria might be useful to him. It was a question of co-ordinating his wishes with an opportunity – which he was able to do in Leiria.

Vítor Pontes was the third man to join the new coach at Leiria, and today he is the only one who isn't working with José Mourinho.

The four of them made up União de Leiria's coaching team for the 2001/2002 season.

In the meantime, the 2000/2001 season was drawing to a close and União de Leiria kept on surprising football fans more and more. They were headed for their best-ever position and, in a final sprint worthy of being recorded for prosperity, they managed to jump from 7th to 5th, 'overtaking' Benfica who, in contrast, registered their worst-ever ranking in 6th place. This put some pressure on José Mourinho's sense of pride. *"It really had an impact on me, and I thought to myself, 'Whatever it takes, I really must do even better. I'm not interested in doing the same; I'm only interested in doing better.'"*

And so he set his sights unimaginably high. So high that it would have been better if he'd kept this to himself and not told anyone, as he'd be taken for a madman. He set out to do better, and better was 4th place, at least.

"Undoubtedly difficult," he thought.

"Undoubtedly impossible," thought someone Mourinho had told of his ambitions for União de Leiria.

> THE DOUBTS OF JOÃO BARTOLOMEU

José Mourinho's experience with Leiria was different and extremely enriching. He was going through a new phase in his life, experiencing new situations. He was living without his family for the first time, as well as living in a city in the centre of Portugal for the first time. The size of the club was also different – different from Sporting, FC Porto, Barcelona or Benfica. As a result of all of this, José Mourinho could wander around the city freely without being approached by the *tiffosi*. The pressure placed on players and coaches can also explain this. In the bigger clubs, the pressure is a lot greater and it has a price. However, according to José Mourinho, in Leiria there is no pressure from the club members. Most of the Leiria members go and watch the matches played at home but *"they also have one ear tuned to the radio to see how Sporting are doing,"* and that says it all.

At the beginning of the pre-season, and with the help of the president, João Bartolomeu, José Mourinho chose a perfect location for the first practices – in the countryside, and not too far from Leiria. João Bartolomeu, a man with a great deal of experience and who'd seen many a season kick off, told Mourinho, *"This place is ideal. It's private and spacious and there's a lot of fresh air. It will be excellent for the players to run in the mountains and valleys around here."*

José Mourinho's reply took João Bartolomeu by surprise – a rather restrained, but nevertheless obvious surprise. *"Mr President, we won't be doing any running here. Our training will be done on the pitch every day, and nowhere else."*

João Bartolomeu insisted, *"Yes, you'll train on the pitch, but in the morning you can run around here."*

Mourinho once again clarified his position: *"No, Mr President, with me no one runs without a ball. There'll be two practices a day and only on the football pitch."*

João Bartolomeu couldn't believe what he was hearing and again insisted: *"But in all the pre-seasons I've seen with all your predecessors, it's normal for the players to run in the woods or on the beach to clean out their lungs."*

Smiling at the look of disbelief and suspicion on the president's face, José Mourinho once again replied, *"Yes, Mr President, but it's best that you understand that if that's how the others worked, then I'm a little different. I don't work that way."*

One of Mourinho's assistant coaches had been listening to the conversation. When João Bartolomeu was no longer within earshot, they exchanged a few words.

"You know what's going to happen when we lose two consecutive games..."

"Of course. He'll immediately say we weren't fit enough."

"That's right."

At that moment, José Mourinho didn't yet know that he would never lose two consecutive matches during his time with União de Leiria.

It was a Saturday, a day off for most people. At the end of their training period, a friendly match had been scheduled. On one team were the technical staff and members of União de Leiria's SAD (Mourinho's bosses). On the other were the journalists, coaches and students who were following the team's pre-season. The match was to take place at the end of that Saturday's practice. However, practice wasn't yet over when Mourinho noticed that the SAD directors were already on the training ground, though on the opposite side, doing their warm-up exercises. Mourinho interrupted the practice at once, and shouting at the 'athletes' who'd started their warm-ups. He told them to get off the pitch. Everyone was surprised. The players and the rest of the technical team said nothing, expecting trouble. The members of União de Leiria's SAD, looked at each other, not quite believing that they were being sent off by a subordinate. With a firm and strong voice, José Mourinho shouted across the pitch, "Get off!" a further three times. Someone retorted, *"But why, Mister? You're training there and we're here. What's the problem?"*

Mourinho would not be dissuaded. *"I'll explain it to you later. Now get off!"*

He shouted across the pitch, 'GET OFF!'

Hesitation gave way to obedience, and União de Leiria had the whole field to themselves for the rest of the practice.

"They had little experience of football, namely professional football and its organisation. So, they must have thought that I was mad for 'chasing' them off the pitch when I didn't need that piece of ground for the practice. They went off the pitch, and at the end I explained that the whole training area was mine, and that in terms of my players' concentration and privacy, it was essential that they had the training grounds to themselves. António Santos Serra was the first to tell me that I was completely right and that it would never happen again."

Later, the assistant coach, Rui Faria, told José Mourinho that he'd thought he would get fired, which wasn't at all convenient as in his whole life he'd only worked for 15 days – exactly the same number of days as União de Leiria's training period up to that point.

But there were still more surprising episodes to come. The next happened soon after and again involved João Bartolomeu, who found the methods used by the trainer he'd just signed a little strange. The season had already started, and União de Leiria made their way up to Paços de Ferreira for an away match.

Mourinho's team won hands down, after an impressive show of attacking football. João Bartolomeu was used to seeing his team play with 3 midfield players, often without a striker and only with fast counter-attack players. Now União de Leiria were different. José Mourinho played with only two midfield players, and in attack he opted for a fixed striker and two outside forwards.

Thus, after the win in Paços de Ferreira, José Mourinho heard of a comment made by João Bartolomeu, expressing his complete surprise with the way the team was being led.

"This coach thinks he's still coaching Benfica; he takes a lot of risks, he plays upfront too much."

From the very beginning, José Mourinho had had an excellent relationship with João Bartolomeu, and so he knew that the remarks made about him were in no way depreciative. However, he did feel that there was some suspicion about the work methods he'd introduced. Although the directors didn't doubt his abilities, they wondered whether the coach, who was used to big clubs, could adapt to one the size of União de Leiria.

This coach thinks he's still coaching Benfica. He plays upfront too much

The answer was to be seen in the results. In the end, Mourinho would leave the club after 19 matches of the season, leaving behind him the best results any coach had ever achieved in Leiria. When he left, União were in fourth place, one point away from being third. If they won the next match against a low-ranking club – which they went on to do – they would go up to third place. Compared to the previous season, Leiria's best ever, José Mourinho managed to lose fewer matches – only 3 – and to increase the number of wins, as well as the points average. In the same period, Leiria also scored more goals and conceded fewer.

But even before these results started pouring in, João Bartolomeu had begun to understand the coach's philosophy. Also, José Mourinho had been very clear when, soon after the league began, he'd said: *"Mr President, in terms of ranking, everything's already been said. The previous season was excellent, and it will be difficult to do better. Without losing sight of this goal, there are other objectives that spur us on. In order to make some money with players at the end of the season, we have to play in such a way that will draw attention to them. So, we have to play like a 'big' team. As a scout for Barcelona, Porto and even Sporting, I know that the scouts who watch us today take into account the game philosophy of the team in which a footballer plays. It immediately gives them a sense of their mindset. No one will come here looking for a striker who only helps the team to defend. If we're talking about a striker, then they want people with an attacking game, and above all an attacking mindset. Basically, scouts need to feel that a player from a 'small' team can transfer to a 'big' team."*

And so the way to play football in Leiria was defined. There was to be no 'big-time' posing, but they were to play 'big'. Reports were handed in to João Bartolomeu on a regular basis, and so responsibility for all manner of risks was assumed. In practical terms, this meant that União de Leiria began to have a different philosophy of the game, as Mourinho explained to his players. *"We have to defend well, as happened last season, but with fewer people; we have to dominate more and be dominated less; we have to counter-attack less and attack more; and we have to score more goals."* In the beginning, it was a little difficult to grasp the new methods and philosophy, but Mourinho had no doubt that they should continue on the path he'd set out.

> CHAMPION WITH 4 PLAYERS FROM LEIRIA

With no pressure from the club members, with the Leiria Board supporting the coach, and with intelligent and skilful players, the months Mourinho spent in Leiria were extremely successful. So successful, that at the end of the first part of the season, Benfica had their eye on him again, as did FC Porto. As we will see, Jorge Nuno Pinto da Costa's prophecy would be fulfilled, just as Mourinho's prophecy had been fulfilled.

In motivating the players, Mourinho had made a promise to the squad at the start. *"Don't doubt that sooner or later I'll go to a big club. And when I go, some of you are coming with me."*

"I never specified who would go with me because that would always depend on the club I would go to. For example, I knew that Benfica needed a left back, and so Nuno Valente was sure he'd go with me. Benfica also needed an outside forward, and Maciel knew too that if I went to Luz, he'd go with me. They knew that some of them would go with me. This situation motivated the players, and at the same time brought us closer together. It was something along the lines 'you help me get there, and then I'll take some of you with me'.

This is how I committed myself to the group – exactly in this way."

Within the group then no one was surprised by the controversial interview he gave to the club's website on the eve of the match against Benfica. When he said that *"with four players from União de Leiria I'd make champions out of Benfica"*, José Mourinho's main objective was to motivate his players, rather than have a dig at Benfica.

"I had no idea those words would take on the gigantic proportions that they did. What I wanted to do was boost my players' morale, not disparage Benfica's players. I only sought to emphasise the quality of the União de Leiria squad, and let them know that they were worthy of playing in any team in Portugal. Obviously I knew we were going to play against Benfica, and so I knew this statement would reach them and could have some sort of effect. But, I repeat, the main objective was to motivate my team."

In the end, after the match against Benfica in Torres Novas, which finished in a draw, Baltemar Brito was the butt of all jokes as the party returned to Leiria.

"In the car park the team-buses of both clubs were parked next to each other. As they share the same colours, they were easily confused. Brito was the first to leave the changing rooms, and he got on the nearest bus. He settled into none other than Jesualdo Ferreira's seat (a Benfica coach), and didn't hold back when he saw the snacks on the seats. He started eating what was probably Jesualdo Ferreira's snack, when all of a sudden he saw the blokes from Benfica getting onto the bus. He only had time to lower his head, think 'what an idiot', and quickly leave the Benfica bus. Obviously, we laughed and joked with Brito all the way from Torres to Leiria, saying things like, 'You already want to go on that bus, do you? Take it easy Brito, you shouldn't draw so much attention to yourself.'"

Except that without knowing it, the coaching staff at União de Leiria were already attracting the attention of the Benfica directors.

> BENFICA ONCE AGAIN

Just before Christmas, on the 16th match of the season, Leiria were playing Farense down in Faro. As usual, the team was in training at the Hotel Montechoro. The afternoon was drawing to a close, the game was the next day, and José Mourinho was in the hotel lobby when his mobile phone rang. It was the agent, José Veiga. He told Mourinho that Toni, the Benfica coach was to be dismissed and – surprise, surprise – José Mourinho was the Board's favourite. According to Veiga, there were past issues that needed resolving, but Mourinho was once again the firm favourite of the Benfica Board. The issues mentioned by José Veiga were of a personal nature, and related to comments that Mourinho had made about the Benfica president when he had left. Nonetheless, it was nothing that couldn't be overcome with the mediation of José Veiga, and even Luís Filipe Vieira.

"I must admit I was a little ruffled, especially because I had a match the next day. I didn't say anything to anybody, but some people immediately realised that something was up, as there were people in Leiria who already knew me well.

However, I told José Veiga that I'd like to work with Benfica again, that my ambition was to go to a big club, but not at any price. Without saying too much, I made it clear that I would only return if I was happy with the terms and conditions, but that I wanted to coach Benfica again. I immediately added that I would want to sign some players, namely Nuno Valente. That signing would be obligatory, and I didn't even mention that Derlei would be another priority. I was told that Benfica could get Nuno Valente, but no one else. Then Veiga also revealed that Jankauskas was hours away from being signed. He obviously asked me to keep this secret, and told me he would contact me again."

José Mourinho remained silent after hanging up. After all, it's not every day that you get a call on behalf of Benfica to be their coach – and in little over a year this was the second one.

"It didn't come as a complete surprise. We all knew that Benfica weren't having a good season, and so Toni's departure was probably just a matter of time. That's the way it is in football; today you're the best and tomorrow

you're a jackass, and vice-versa. Despite all the problems there were when I left Benfica, I knew that no one had questioned my competence, and so that was the strongest indicator that I might be able to return one day."

The next day União de Leiria beat Faro. Christmas was just around the corner, and José Mourinho tried not to think any more about the call from José Veiga. He enjoyed a peaceful Christmas, then it was back to routine competition.

Leiria were riding high. Blazing a trail that was remarkable in every way, the team were now preparing for their next two matches, both home fixtures.

Before the match on Boxing Day, José Mourinho was invited to go to Lisbon for a more concrete encounter. It was the first time he'd had any contact with Manuel Vilarinho since leaving Benfica. It was thought that this meeting should take place between the two of them alone – in order to bury the hatchet.

Accompanied by assistant coach Baltemar Brito, José Mourinho made his way to the capital. He parked in front of Vilarinho's house. As he got out of the car, he saw the Benfica president's Mercedes jeep pull up alongside him. When Manuel Vilarinho got out of the jeep, people walking by spotted them, and the surprise on their faces clearly showed that they had recognised both president and coach. They went up to the second floor of a building in a narrow street 'adorned' with bars, where music and youth reign supreme. With Manuel Vilarinho leading the way, they stepped into a spacious room, decorated in unquestionably good taste. The family photographs and personal objects immediately revealed that this was the office of the Benfica president.

Courteous words had already been exchanged, and now they moved on to the main subject in hand: the past.

"We quickly got talking about what conclusions we could come to. We were more interested in discussing ways to get over the past, than in going over what had happened. As we swapped versions of events, we realised that much of what had been said and done stemmed from misunderstandings. As far as I'm concerned, I came to the conclusion that – as I told Manuel Vilarinho – I'd been influenced by some people's versions, which probably didn't coincide with the facts. I also regretted certain 'loaded' sentences – for example, when I said that 'Vilarinho had no say in Benfica.' That conversation was 'almost' an apology on both sides. Today, looking back, I think that even though I didn't go back to Benfica, that meeting was extremely positive as we cleared up a great many things. That's when I concluded, with certainty, that Manuel Vilarinho is a good man. I wish him all the best on a personal level; and as for football-related issues, as long as his interests don't clash with mine, I wish him every success."

Once they'd got problems of a personal nature out of the way, they began discussing the future. That's when the first differences came up.

"The first obstacle that came up was Jesualdo Ferreira. And why? Because we started talking about the players I thought were needed in order to take on the rest of the league, as well as the coaching staff I wanted. At this point, Manuel Vilarinho told me that Jesualdo Ferreira would have to continue as assistant coach, given the respect he deserved and the commitment Vilarinho had undertaken when he'd signed him from Alverca. At that very moment, all negotiation was over for me. I told Manuel Vilarinho, in no uncertain terms, that with Jesualdo Ferreira as assistant, I would never be Benfica's coach. I thanked him from the bottom of my heart for the fact that we had overcome the barrier between us, but as for the future, I wouldn't be the coach at Luz under the conditions he'd presented."

That conversation with Vilanrinho was almost an apology on both sides

Although it hadn't been an easy decision, Mourinho had taken it quickly.

His ideas were clear and some of them couldn't be changed. All in all, he was following the path he'd mapped out for himself since the first day of his professional life. His ambition was to go as far as he could in his chosen profession, but not at any price. His principles were untouchable, as was his loyalty.

"I didn't want Jesualdo Ferreira at all, because I had very well defined ideas about my coaching staff. Baltemar Brito and Rui Faria would surely go with me when I left União de Leiria. Furthermore, Benfica also had a goalkeeper coach, the Iraqi Samir, who'd stay on until the end of the season, at least. In theory, he'd then be replaced either by Vítor Pontes from União de Leiria, or by Silvino from FC Porto. I also wanted Carlos Mozer to return. Faced with all of this, I couldn't see where to place Jesualdo Ferreira. It was clear to me that both his past, and the path he'd forged as head coach called for great care when dealing with this case. I couldn't give him a lower-ranking post, but at the same time I had no post suited to his profile. I did, however, make it clear that I had no problem with Jesualdo Ferreira staying on at Benfica, as long as it wasn't in the club's Technical Department."

The first obstacle that came up was Jesualdo Ferreira

Manuel Vilarinho was now aware of José Mourinho's reasons for not wanting to work with Jesualdo Ferreira. Informed, but not convinced.

"I believe Manuel Vilarinho thought that a coach from União de Leiria would never turn down an offer from Benfica, and that despite my firm reply, I would end up giving in. However, if that was the case, he was completely mistaken. As far as I was concerned, negotiations were over – but not for Manuel Vilarinho. He told me we would speak again, and that this situation would be overcome by Luís Filipe Vieira."

Convinced that the obstacle had to be overcome, but by Manuel Vilarinho giving in, Mourinho headed back to Leiria. When he got back to his car, Baltemar Brito was still waiting for him. José Mourinho immediately told him, *"It's over; we're not going to Benfica."* Then he explained the insurmountable difference that he had with the club's president.

> LUÍS FILIPE VIEIRA STEPS UP THE PRESSURE

The next day, there were further developments. José Veiga phoned José Mourinho first thing in the morning, telling him that even though he was in Luxembourg over the Christmas period, negotiations would carry on. He then asked Mourinho to return to Lisbon to his own office, where he was to meet Carlos Janela, his assistant, and Luís Filipe Vieira. When José Mourinho expressed his doubts as to the usefulness of new contacts, Veiga replied, *"Go, the Jesualdo issue will be sorted out. Don't worry."*

More out of courtesy than a belief in what Veiga had said, José Mourinho set off the same day to Lisbon, accompanied once more by Baltemar Brito, as well as Rui Faria. In Lisbon, they got out of the coach's Volvo and crossed the street before going their separate ways. Mourinho was headed for the meeting, and his assistant coaches to dinner. In the middle of the street, they were almost run over by António Bastos, none other than one of the vice-presidents of União de Leiria. Bastos stopped, and Mourinho joked, *"Mr Bastos, can you picture it? Tomorrow's front pages will read 'Leiria's vice-president runs over coaches.'"* António Bastos also joined in the joke and then continued on his way. Less than ten minutes later, João Bartolomeu was on the phone to Mourinho. Bartolomeu knew very well where Veiga's office was, and he knew something was up.

"So, Mourinho, where are you going? To Benfica? I know you're close to José Veiga's office..."

José Mourinho knew it was impossible to fool the União de Leiria president. He didn't deny or confirm anything, but he made the following promise.

"Mr President, rest assured that for now I'm not going anywhere and if I do, I won't do anything without informing you."

There was a fundamental reason for this reply. José Mourinho was totally convinced that there'd be no getting round the issue that was holding up negotiations.

Mourinho knew Veiga's office well. Leather couches, modern furniture and various paintings – all depicting sports themes – created an atmosphere of harmony and elegance in the spacious room where the second meeting was to be held. When he arrived, Carlos Janela and Luís Filipe Vieira were already waiting for him.

Luís Filipe Vieira went straight to the matter in hand. Once again they reached a stalemate regarding the assistant coach. Filipe Vieira paid Jesualdo Ferreira 'a thousand and one' compliments. To him it was clear that Jesualdo Ferreira – a man of his confidence, a man from Benfica and an honest man – would work with any coach without creating any problems. Jesualdo had only one aim: to help. Luís Filipe Vieira also raised a moral question. He could not forget that he had brought Jesualdo Ferreira to Benfica, when the latter was in a very comfortable position in Alverca. For that reason, he couldn't now simply abandon him.

Filipe Vieira then paid Jesualdo Ferreira a thousand and one compliments

Quietly, José Mourinho listened to the reasons put forward by Vieira. At the end, he gave him a choice.

"I either tell Jesualdo Ferreira, face to face, that I don't want to work with him, so that he clearly understands that I am the one who doesn't want to work with him; or that's the end of it, and I won't go to Benfica."

At around this point, a call came in from a Benfica director who, realising that they were still at an impasse, made the following suggestion: *"Why doesn't Mourinho accept him as an assistant coach and then start marginalizing him from the very beginning, so that Jesualdo understands what's going on and chooses to leave?"*

Today, out of respect for Jesualdo Ferreira, José Mourinho still does not wish to divulge the name of that 'scheming' Benfica director.

Perturbed and rather uncomfortable with this new possibility, Mourinho would hear no more and brought negotiations with the Benfica directors to a close, for the second time. Once again, he headed towards Leiria. He told Baltemar Brito and Rui Faria everything that had gone on in Veiga's office, and the three were certain that the Benfica chapter had been closed.

>> CHAPTER IV **PREPARING THE FUTURE**

FC PORTO 2001/02

PINTO DA COSTA SPEAKS
WE'LL BE CHAMPIONS NEXT YEAR
THE WORST PORTO IN THE LAST 26 YEARS
MOURINHO'S DOUBT AND VILARINHO'S DREAM
ONLY A GUN WILL STOP REAL MADRID
A BITTER PILL FOR THE DRAGONS TO SWALLOW
THE POSTIGA SOAP OPERA BEGINS
THE NIGHTMARE RETURNS
ON TRACK FOR THE UEFA CUP
JOSÉ MOURINHO'S 'BIBLE'

>> CHAP. IV **PREPARING THE FUTURE**

On 28 December 2001, José Mourinho received a phone call from Baideck.

It was the first of several contacts made by FC Porto to try to prevent Mourinho returning to Benfica, and to make an undertaking to the 'dragons' [11] instead.

There's no one better than Jorge Nuno Pinto da Costa, FC Porto's charismatic president, to explain why and how things happened.

> *PINTO DA COSTA SPEAKS*

Why Mourinho?

In football, as indeed in any other activity, there are always two possibilities facing the decision-maker: the decision will either work, or not. This incredibly obvious truth comes from 'La Palisse'.

People like me, presidents of football clubs, have the responsibility to choose a head coach for our teams, and so we are subject to being 'spot on', or 'way off base'. It is always a 'subjective' decision, and only the results will prove 'objectively' whether or not we chose well.

As always, at the beginning of the 2001/2002 season we made our choice, hoping that, despite being hotly contested, it would be a positive one both in terms of the quality of play and the results.

However, play hadn't improved and neither had results.

Unfortunately, in December, we had four bad results, within a space of eighteen days:

1-0 to Sparta Prague; 2-0 to Vitória de Guimarães; 0–0 to Sporting de Braga; and 2-1 to Santa Clara.

For a club that was used to winning, this was obviously bad and morale was down. We were in 5th place in the League table.

At around this time, Christmas 2001, José Mourinho's star was shining brightly and he had put União de Leiria ahead of FC Porto. It was almost certain

11. *The Dragon is the symbol of FC Porto*

that he would go back to Benfica. That would have been even worse for us; I was well aware that his worth, courage and ambition could lead any team to success.

I contacted a mutual friend, Jorge Baideck, and asked if there was any truth about Mourinho's imminent return to Benfica. He said 'yes', but that it was Mourinho's dream to return to FC Porto as head coach. I drew Baideck's attention to the fact that we already had a coach, and that I'd do everything to keep him on. Nevertheless, Jorge Baideck insisted on a meeting between us the next day. It was 27 December, and the next day wasn't very convenient as it was my birthday.

But a meeting was indeed necessary, as I was informed that on 29 December, at 6:00 pm, Benfica intended to introduce Mourinho as their head coach.

We decided, then, that they would both come to my house at around midnight, and be shown in as soon as the last guest had left. At midnight, they were close by my house, but they would have to wait until two in the morning because that's when the party came to an end, despite my yawning several times to show that I was tired and sleepy.

After the customary hug between friends who have met up once more, I was brought up to date as to where things stood. I emphasised the fact that José Mourinho knew I meant to keep the same coach and that I would do everything to ensure this would happen. So, given this situation, I only left him with a single guarantee. *"You will succeed Octávio in FC Porto, but only at the end of his contract."*

Mourinho's eyes sparkled and he shook my hand, saying, *"I'll stay on at Leiria and expect not to come to FC Porto this year, then."*

We had a glass of champagne and spoke of a shared past full of good memories. It was almost daybreak when Mourinho left to oversee a training match at União de Leiria, and despite the Lisbon newspapers announcing to all that Mourinho would be the Benfica coach, he was still with Leiria.

I remember that the headline in that day's *Record* [12] read *'MOURINHO IS THE CHOSEN ONE'*.

Life went on as usual, but if December had been a bad month for us, then January was even worse. Between 12 and 19 January we put paid to any hopes we had of making it to the Champions League when we drew at home against Sporting, and lost 2-0 at Bessa Stadium. Also, we didn't make it to the final of the Portuguese Cup, as we had lost at home to Sporting de Braga – who were themselves eliminated later by Leixões.

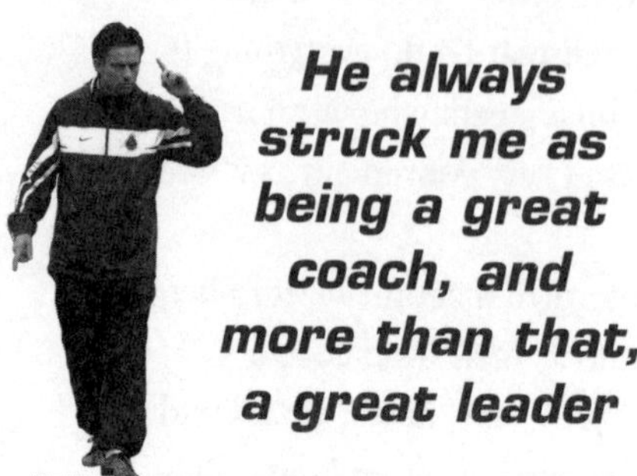

He always struck me as being a great coach, and more than that, a great leader

This situation could not continue, and the coach resigned by mutual agreement.

After difficult, but proper negotiations with the Board of União de Leiria/SAD, José Mourinho was not only our chosen one, he was in fact FC Porto's head coach.

Why? Essentially, because it was my dream! How many coaches, based on nothing concrete, would turn down a contract with a big club, simply on a handshake, to sign with another club who knows when?

He'd always struck me as being a great coach, and more than that, as a great leader. And his best calling card and the most accurate reflection of his personality was when he introduced himself to the players, saying *"We'll be champions next year"*.

Everything was summed up by that single sentence: confidence, determination and the desire to convey his unshakable will to win.

His work will be remembered.

As for his future, we – his friends – all hope that it will be what he deserves. Given his strength as a coach, his humanity, his love of family, his honesty and loyalty, we trust he will continue to make us all very happy as we see ourselves reflected in his success.

Jorge Nuno Pinto da Costa
President of FC Porto

12. A Portuguese sports newspaper dedicated to football

> WE'LL BE CHAMPIONS NEXT YEAR

On 23 January 2002, José Mourinho was introduced as FC Porto's head coach. At a press conference packed with journalists, both the new coach and the president Jorge Nuno Pinto da Costa explained the reasons leading to Mourinho's move to Antas. Much was said that day, and there were many questions and answers. However, one sentence from José Mourinho made headlines in all the papers the next day.

"We'll be champions next year" was the statement that everybody was writing about. FC Porto had won many titles over the previous two decades, and thus its recent history undoubtedly made it possible for the new coach not only to dream, but even to promise they'd win the 2002/2003 season – a season where he'd be solely responsible for selecting the players. Full of confidence in his own abilities, and because *"the FC Porto team was on its deathbed at that time"*, José Mourinho wanted the Porto supporters to know right from the very beginning that he was there to win. He never imagined that a single sentence – with the sole intention of raising people's spirits – would generate so much controversy, hatred and envy. But the promise had been made and Mourinho was faced with only one option: he had to win with FC Porto. In this way, the 'Porto flag' had been hoisted on the main flagpole at Antas Stadium, and Mourinho wanted to unite the entire blue-and-white [13] 'nation' around the new flag from the outset.

As for the season under way, his objectives were much more restrained. As things didn't depend solely on him – the team was ranked sixth in the First Division, and Sporting de Braga had put them out of the running for the Portuguese Cup – Mourinho didn't mind taking a risk.

"I'd like us to try to win this season. However, this no longer depends on us, but rather on third parties. Winning isn't enough. We need to start accumulating points, starting on Saturday with the match against Marítimo."

But more promises were still to come. The journalists wanted to know how FC Porto would play from that point on. José Mourinho left those at the press conference in no doubt.

"I promise that I intend to play on the attack. I promise that we will work towards that goal every day, until we reach a perfectly systematic and

13. *Blue and white are the colours worn by FC Porto*

automatic model. When that day comes, I promise you attacking football; until then, I promise that I deliberately intend to attack."

As for how he would do so, i.e. his game philosophy, once again the coach left no room for misinterpretations.

"Today, the players have already begun to understand my philosophy. You need go no further – simply analyse the way my former club plays. União de Leiria have played in a certain way, according to a predominantly attacking model. With players of the stature of FC Porto, it would not make sense to transform an attacking philosophy into a more defensive model. The very characteristics of these players set us on a specific path, which will never include a defensive way of playing."

In short, José Mourinho promised an attack-minded FC Porto in order to become a winning FC Porto. Sitting next to him, Jorge Nuno Pinto da Costa also looked to the future. *"Our confidence in his worth knows no bounds. He will represent a turning point for FC Porto."* To the chagrin of their opponents and foes, both men would be proven right. Not only did FC Porto make a 'turn-round', they also went on to be champions. In fact, one thing is linked to the other.

However, other promises were made in the changing rooms. When he got there, José Mourinho's speech wasn't very different to the one he'd made back in Benfica. After all, if it had worked once, it could work again. What was important, once again, was to make the rules of the game clear to everyone and to motivate his new 'tribe'.

"Upon my first meeting with the players, I promised them quality work on my part, and I told them that the team would soon be better. I also told them that they would all be valued and that they'd be better in the future. I was aware of the impact my work methods would have on the players."

FC Porto hadn't won any championship for three years. José Mourinho knew that he was coming in at a decisive time. He also knew, however, that there were several factors in his favour. On the one hand, there was a president you could count on beyond the call of duty. On the other hand, after several matches played at Antas – as coach for União de Leiria and assistant coach for Barcelona – he knew of the tremendous affection that the demanding Porto supporters and fans had for him. José Mourinho thus realised that there was a great deal of support, which would allow him a reasonable margin of error. But some things had to be changed. For starters, the songs at Antas.

I was faced with men who had been overwhelmed by defeat

"The songs were terrible for the Porto players themselves. In the stands, the fans would sing things like: 'play ball, you clowns, play ball' or 'you're a disgrace, you're all a disgrace'. The players themselves sometimes still sing these songs today in order to remember times they can't go back to."

Nevertheless, Mourinho and the players know that those songs and lyrics are still sung today – but now someone else is on the receiving end. Early on, they started to be aimed at the FC Porto opponents who made their way to Antas, and constituted an element of anti-football.

> THE WORST PORTO IN 26 YEARS

At the press conference, José Mourinho had hinted that Porto could still try to win the League. However, deep down, he didn't believe it was possible.

"I found a Porto made up of players who were very different to those I'd left behind when Robson and I moved to Barcelona. Ambition was nowhere close to what it had been in the past, which surprised me somewhat given what I knew about the club. I believe that a football team is only worthy of being called that when every single player, without exception, wants to win – and wants to win a great deal, regardless of whether or not he is playing. At Antas, I came across a group of players with very different personalities. I was faced with men who had been overwhelmed by defeat. As an example of this, I remember Paredes, among others. On the other hand, I also saw players who were happy with the life they were leading. They belonged to a club that paid them well, without fail, and which offered them good working conditions. Also, they were living in a city where any family feels comfortable. Thus, winning or losing were the same to them, as was getting any titles. Those players made it onto my list of players to be released, and no longer play for Porto today. For all these reasons, I never believed Porto would win the League in the year that I arrived. That wasn't my team, and there were very few players I could count on."

That is why Mourinho was very clear in an interview to a Spanish paper when he said, *"This is the worst Porto in the last 26 years."* But the players weren't the only ones at fault.

"I think the president, Pinto da Costa, won't hold this analysis against me. The moment FC Porto left behind its traditional model and became a SAD [14]*, it moved towards a new management model, where power was no longer totally centred round the president and head coach. New positions were created for a director-oriented structure, which resulted in the decentralisation of power. In my opinion, the key to Porto's success lay precisely, as I said, in the centralised power of the president and head coach. On the other hand, up until then the club had been financially stable – but only just. This stability was reflected in extremely strict policies regarding the signing, loan transfer and release of players. Upon the creation of SAD, and*

14. *SAD: Sociedade Anónima Desportiva – a public limited company (football club).*

given an increase in capital a few years later, the club had never been in a better financial position. This situation, together with certain structural changes, allowed the club to think differently. And I believe the results were clear for everyone to see: money was spent and players were signed without the due attention, concern and rigour of those who cannot afford to fail. This was a normal course to follow, but it led to some sporting and management errors. Signing Ibarra, Pizzi and Esnaider are practical examples that support my analysis."

With his eye on the next season, José Mourinho soon started to put his strategy into practice.

"I was faced with a dilemma. Should I grab hold of ten or twelve players – those who would move into the next season with me – and start working with them seriously, focusing on the future; or should I motivate the entire group and try to make those who weren't in line with my methods fit in better?"

Irrespective of his decision, none of this would happen overnight. And while thought was being given to major decisions – although none had as yet been taken – Porto won four consecutive matches in the League after Mourinho's arrival, and were once again on track to win the League, and this was now being said in the press. Although he kept silent, Mourinho didn't entirely share this opinion.

"When a coach begins his work halfway through the season, he can always make one of two choices. He can opt for a psychological beating – which I don't believe in – or he can choose a methodological beating. The former is purely related to the effects brought about by changing coach. These are only short-term effects because players are affected on a psychological level. It is a time when everyone wants to prove something to the new coach, but it is no longer effective when things begin to be defined in terms of 'who plays and who doesn't, who's sent to the bench and who isn't'. At this point, the coach can then make a choice. He is either lulled and everything remains the same, or he opts for the methodological beating which, on the contrary, produces long-lasting effects because it brings about structural changes. In this case, changes in the work philosophy and the model of play can be seen."

José Mourinho wasn't taken in by the wins at home, against Marítimo (2-1) and Benfica (3-2), and away, against Varzim (1-0) and Vitória de Setúbal (4-1).

However, he needed to convey a certain message to those outside. On matchday twenty-three, Porto were in 3rd place – five points behind Sporting, in first place. There was no way he could give up the fight for first place. Anything could happen and José Mourinho decided to motivate his players. *"It is still possible"* or *"I was wrong; the squad is better than I thought"* were phrases that began to be read in the papers.

> MOURINHO'S DOUBTS & VILARINHO'S DREAM

One of the decisive moments in this initial phase was the match against Benfica. Both clubs were equal third, and a loss at home could seriously affect Porto's chances of making it to the UEFA Cup the following year.

When preparing for the game, José Mourinho was beset by doubts.

"I didn't know how Benfica would play in terms of attack. Would they opt for a fixed striker (Jankauskas) and two outside forwards (Mantorras and Simão Saborosa), or would they place Mantorras in the middle with Miguel and Carlitos on the wings? I needed to know. If Jankauskas played, I would have Ricardo Silva marking him because he defends high balls well. However, against Mantorras I would choose Ricardo Costa, a midfielder who is very quick at recovering the ball."

The difficulty lay in knowing what option Jesualdo Ferreira would choose for the match. A master of pragmatism, José Mourinho resorted to the 'spy' he'd used before at Luz Stadium, when working for Benfica. This time the 'spy' would act against Benfica. After watching some training practices and speaking to various observers of the practices at Luz, Mourinho's spy sent his final report to the FC Porto trainer.

"There was no scrimmage or tactical training, but from the exercises they carried out, and from one or other dead ball situation that they practised, as well as from the way the players were grouped in certain reduced situations, I strongly believe Jankauskas will be the one to play."

From that moment on, Mourinho started preparing Ricardo Silva to take on Benfica and to mark the Lithuanian striker.

In this way, José Mourinho was getting ready for the match against Benfica, when Manuel Vilarinho's 'dream' made headlines. The Benfica president confessed to journalists that he had dreamt his club would beat Porto at Antas... by 3-0.

Once more Mourinho got the strength he needed from his adversary.

"I had decided not to make any declarations that week that might upset the normal course of training for my players. However, I didn't take too kindly to Manuel Vilarinho's 'dream'. As far as I am concerned, not even in dreams would I have the audacity to think that I would go to my opponents' home ground and win 3-0. When Vilarinho made his 'dream' known to the public, I immediately thought that there was the 'provocation' I needed to shake up my players' pride. At once, I had a photocopy taken of the interview with Vilarinho, and I put it up on the wall in the changing rooms at Antas for the whole week, so that nobody would forget Vilarinho's 'dream'. The only thing I told the papers was that 'nobody beats us 3-0 on our home ground'. And we went into that match feeling somewhat spurred on."

I had a photocopy made of the interview with Vilarinho and put it up in Porto's changing rooms

The game didn't get off to an easy start. Benfica scored right at the beginning, and only a goal by Deco towards the end of the first half gave the team some stability. At half-time, José Mourinho spoke to the players and felt he'd accomplished something.

"In the middle of the changing rooms at Antas there is a huge basket, into which the players throw all their dirty laundry, towels, socks, cups, etc. When I walked in I was furious because I felt that nobody on my team, apart from Deco, wanted to 'take the game by the horns' and take charge of it. They played as if the ball burnt their feet, and I couldn't accept this, as this was the first step towards losing the match. When I walked into the changing rooms, I kicked the basket and everything fell out. The basket flew into the air, and suddenly I saw Vítor Baía step in to 'save' it. Then I spoke about tactics for a minute, and about history for another nine minutes. The history of both clubs and the history of the derby. I told them to their faces, 'We're closer to losing this game, than to winning it. Do you know how long it's been since they won

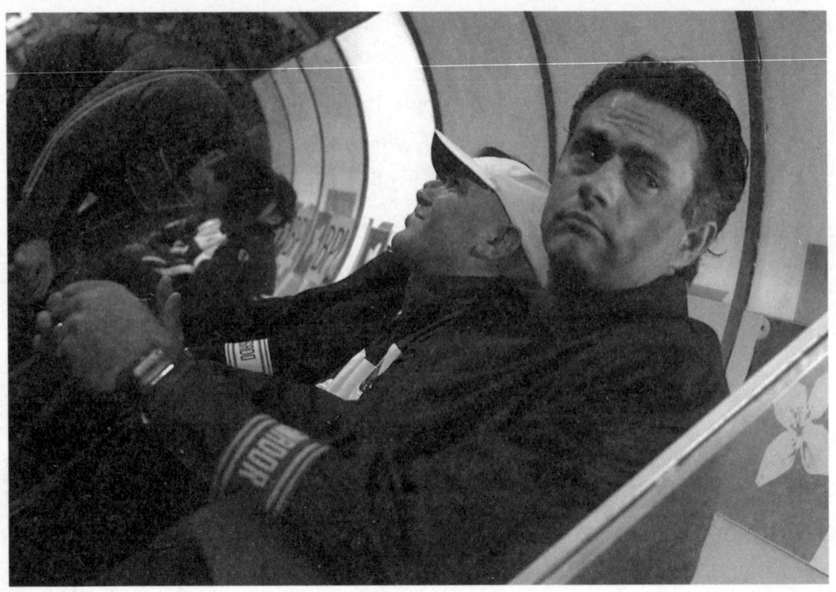

a match at Antas? Do you want to go down in history for losing against Benfica in this stadium after so many years?'

Then I asked Zé Luís, the masseur, who'd been with the club for over 50 years, how many times Benfica had won there. Without answering, he looked at me sheepishly. Then I asked Vítor Baía the same question. He replied they had lost against Benfica at Antas just once, over ten years before.

I felt that everything I had told them was working. I saw them start motivating each other, and it was then that I thought we still had plenty of time to win the game."

Mourinho took Pavlin off and sent Alenitchev on. The second half was completely different and FC Porto scored two goals straight away, allowing them to control the rest of the match. The final score was 3-2. The following day, the papers and Porto fans alike were abuzz with something José Mourinho had said: *"We could have thrashed them."*

The next matchday saw Porto beat Setúbal 4-1, and bring to a close a cycle of four consecutive wins. With Benfica slipping and motivation levels ever higher at Porto, it was time to think that winning the League was within their reach. However, this proved to be nothing more than a short-lived mirage.

> ONLY A GUN WILL STOP REAL MADRID

Back in the running for the League, José Mourinho now had the chance to put the team in contention for the Champions League, as they strove towards the quarter-finals. But this was to be an extremely difficult task, as FC Porto were off to the Bernabeu Stadium to play Real Madrid. Before the match, one of José Mourinho's comments grabbed everyone's attention: *"Only a gun will stop Real Madrid."* In saying so, he had meant to take off some of the pressure that the Porto players were feeling, as they were about to face what was probably the best team in the world. On the other hand, Mourinho firmly believes that a theoretically weaker team should be humble and never provoke the stronger one, so as to take advantage of the possibility that their opponents might be 'asleep'. But football is also about having fun, and José Mourinho himself wanted to relax and joke a little with his assistants. And the humour didn't stop there.

"A strange thing happened as my technical team and I were preparing tactically for the game. When we put pen to paper to draw up the plan for the match, we realised that we would need 13 players to beat Real. Their team was made up of: Castillas, Michel Salgado, Hierro, Kaanka and Roberto Carlos; Figo, Helguera, Makelele and Zidane; Gutti and Morientes. In order to have an effective team, I came to the following conclusion: I should have a player to mark Morientes and a free midfielder close behind; another player to mark Figo and yet another in the area he frees up with his diagonal passes, which allows other players into this corridor; I'd need a player to mark Zidane, but as he plays out of his area a great deal, I'd have to have a right full back to occupy that space; finally as I always play with three forwards, I'd need to keep them, too. If we added it all up, including the other players I usually play with, we would have 13 players in order to beat Real Madrid. As the referee didn't allow this, we only played with eleven players and we lost 1-0."

In any case, FC Porto put on a great performance, and a draw – or even a win – would have been a more accurate reflection of what both teams produced during the ninety minutes of play.

The Porto supporters thus turned their attention to the Portuguese League and their first loss came immediately after, against Beira-Mar. José Mourinho witnessed his team lose 3-2 at home, and in this way definitely lay to rest the 'feeling' of fighting for the title. Today, the pragmatic coach says, *"That team – which wasn't a team in the real sense of the word – once more brought to the surface all the weaknesses I had detected upon my arrival."*

Another defeat at Antas Stadium lay in store four days later. Porto were to host Real Madrid this time, and would once again have to play without a gun and with 'only' eleven players. The Porto fans lost hope early on in the match, as nineteen minutes into the game Mourinho's pupils were already down 2-0. Capucho still managed to score for Porto before half-time, but one goal wasn't enough and the team of Vicente del Bosque again defeated them, this time 2-1. With the team clearly on a downward spiral, José Mourinho gave a warning at the end of the match: *"I'm going to have to find players who are mentally strong in this squad."*

At the same time, his ideas about the following season were becoming increasingly clear. And so, initial contacts were made with certain players – or with their agents – and the respective clubs. Some of those contacted, either directly or indirectly, included: Maniche, Pedro Emanuel, Paulo Ferreira, Derlei and Nuno Valente. The names of Jankauskas and César Peixoto would crop up later.

> A BITTER PILL TO SWALLOW

After three consecutive defeats, FC Porto made their way to the now-defunct Vidal Pinheiro stadium to play against Salgueiros. The 3-0 win brought back some peace of mind to the team, which had by now lowered its sights – as had José Mourinho in his comments to the press. Their objectives were now to consolidate their third place and qualify for the UEFA Cup.

Belenenses were their next opponents, and on 9 March 2002 the headline in the newspaper *Comércio do Porto* was *"A bitter pill for the dragons to swallow"*. An unbelievable 3-0 defeat for Porto. Even today, José Mourinho feels that the match in Restelo was the worst game he ever saw FC Porto play as the team's coach. At this point great tension arose between José Mourinho and most of his players. The coach was to prove once again that he could take away just as easily as he had given.

So, José Mourinho broke one of his golden rules: the one not to 'burden' players with speeches at the end of matches. For the first and only time, the coach spoke to his players at the end of a football match.

It was at this point that great tension was felt by most of the players for the first time

"I was very hard on them, but the game was bad beyond belief. I told them that I was prepared to change everything and, if necessary, I would – there and then – stop counting on those players that as far as I was concerned could leave at any moment. I emphasised that the game had been a disgrace, and then went even further by telling them that if I were to go down in the club's history as the coach who at the end of so many years had failed to qualify for European competition, then so be it. In the meantime, things would either change very quickly or, if need be, I would even have the juniors play. All in all, I let rip, because I felt that my players hadn't given their all on the pitch.

They listened to me in silence, and I got the feeling that they had understood that if they didn't change their attitude, I really would go through with what I was saying!"

At the press conference after the match, José Mourinho said, *"There are players in this squad who will get me nowhere."* He didn't mention their names, but everyone knew who he was talking about when a few months later FC Porto announced the list of players to be released. But it was at that point that radical changes were made and the foundations were laid for the FC Porto of the future. He finally answered the question he'd asked himself upon his arrival at Porto, and after the game at Restelo he began to think of the future, working with those players who were to stay in the squad. That's when the final selection was made, and José Mourinho clearly understood which of his players were strong and psyched up for 'battle', and which weren't.

"After that game, I also told them that it was up to the club members to call

them whatever they liked the next day. The members had that right. They, however, did not have the right to play the way they had against Belenenses. I told them all this, and then said the same thing to the journalists."

FC Porto would not lose another match in the First Division for the remainder of the 2001/2002 season.

> THE POSTIGA SOAP OPERA BEGINS

Hélder Postiga was a key player in the FC Porto shaped by José Mourinho. However, the two men fought a long, and sometimes hard, secret battle. Their relationship wasn't always easy – at times aggressive, at others supportive, they often came close to going their separate ways.

The first conflict between them arose at the end of the match against Belenenses. Hélder Postiga had been sent off, and ended up being on the receiving end of José Mourinho's anger. As always, he listened in silence, without uttering a single word. José Mourinho thought that his sending off was unthinkable for a professional footballer.

"Hélder was sent off when we were down 1-0. The game was already going badly for us, and it got even worse with one less player. I was furious and I told him that he wouldn't play with me again. I said that I didn't want players like that on my team, and that he was straight on his way to the B team, etc, etc. He listened silently and said nothing because he is a very polite kid; he's introverted, shy even. It was our first 'war', and many others were to follow. Hélder has a great deal of potential, and if he chooses to listen to others, he can go very far in world football. In the meantime, he still has a lot to learn, and I won't give up teaching him.

I am sure that a few years from now, when he is rich, with lots of titles under his belt and many goals, he'll tell somebody – his wife or kids, if he has some – that 'that guy was an almighty pain, but he liked me and he helped me to grow. I must thank him'.

Even today, I think he feels I am his greatest enemy and there are days that he can't bear to hear the sound of my voice. I have the distinct feeling that there are times when he is looking at me, listening and thinking 'here is this

son of a gun, bugging me again.' But I am also sure that one day he'll understand why I'm so hard on him, and as I said, he'll tell someone or even me, 'Thank you'."

> THE NIGHTMARE RETURNS

Four days after their defeat in Belém, and in torrential rain, FC Porto welcomed the Greek team, Panathinaikos. Mourinho made six changes to his initial line-up, with only one – the replacement of Vítor Baía by Paulo Santos – due to injury. All the other changes were his decision.

There were very few spectators to watch the 'blue-and-white' 2-1 win, which eased the tension a little and kept hopes alive of qualifying for the Champions League. It was the team's first triumph in the second phase of UEFA's most important competition, and José Mourinho felt that *"the players had had a good attitude"*.

In theory, the next match for the Portuguese League could be won and would boost morale. FC Porto were at home to Alverca – a club that would drop to the second division at the end of the season – but Porto only managed to draw 1-1. The nightmare continued and José Mourinho broke with certain players once and for all.

"I told them that regardless of what they might do until the end of the championship, I no longer counted on them. That was a given. Another given was the group I would be counting on for the next year. There was also a third group, but I hadn't made any decisions about these players yet. Without

mentioning any names, I said all of this to the squad. However, I made it clear that the door to my office was open to any player who wanted to know which of the three groups he belonged to. Few players dropped by.

For this reason, and several others, we went through a period of some emotional instability. I remember a player who was 'sentenced' for an incident that marked both the group and me. During a practice, I reprimanded him severely for not agreeing with certain tactical training points, namely his position on the field. This happened towards the end of the training session, but I had already forgotten all about it by the end of the practice.

The president, Pinto da Costa, usually came down to see me at the end of each practice, and I was already in my office that day when, three or four minutes after the training session, he walked in.

'So, Mister, I already know that you had a problem with a player today!'

I was completely taken aback by how fast news got round.

'You know? How do you know?'

'Because as soon as the player walked into the changing rooms, he phoned his agent to tell him what had happened, and the agent then told someone else who, in turn, told me.'

In the light of this information, both the president and I started laughing, as both of us knew who we were dealing with and how this case would end."

That weakness of spirit, attitude and mentality had to come to an end

The player in question was released on loan, and so missed out on a great season filled with victories.

Alverca were the next opponents. Everyone knew that 'Europe' was at stake, and that we could lose everything at the slightest slip-up. Benfica were on the lookout and wouldn't quit. A draw against Alverca meant that the team dropped to fourth place, and didn't qualify for the UEFA Cup. Unswayable in his convictions, Mourinho fearlessly continued stopping using certain players. The UEFA Cup might be the price to pay, but it had to be done for the sake of the future.

The immediate future was Prague. It was all or nothing, in a match where nothing seemed the most probable outcome. In order to qualify for the UEFA Cup, Porto had to beat Sparta Prague and hope that Real would beat Panathinaikos in Greece. Not only did the Spanish not win, but Porto also lost, 2-0. The headline in the *Jornal de Notícias* [15] read *'An inglorious goodbye'*. In turn, José Mourinho, who used players like Pavlin, Pena, Ibarra, Ricardo Silva and Paulo Santos in the line-up for the last time, told journalists that *"it was unbelievably bad… but it was true"*.

"On the way back from Prague, I remember sitting next to the president, Pinto da Costa, and talking about the match. We both agreed wholeheartedly that that lack of spirit, attitude, mentality and cohesion had to come to an end, as had that team. Thus, there was no turning back in terms of the changes that we were carrying out, and it would be best to risk everything, once and for all, and change mentalities, thereby breaking with the team's past – even if that meant we wouldn't make it to the UEFA Cup."

After the match in Prague, there was little time to prepare for the following game against União de Leiria. Nevertheless, there was enough time to make some changes.

For example, Joca was brought into the first eleven for the first time, and Pedro Oliveira from the B team also made his debut.

However, these changes weren't reflected in results and a 1-1 draw took FC Porto even further away from third place. Nevertheless, the way was being paved for the future.

"I can say that the team which played against União de Leiria was my team. Almost all the players who played in that game were part of the squad that went on to win the Champions League: Secretário, Ricardo Carvalho, Jorge Andrade (he left because he was sold, but I was counting on him), Mário Silva, Paredes (the same situation as Jorge Andrade), Joca, Cândido Costa, Clayton and Hélder Postiga. At a time when I'd broken off with so many players and had clearly shown the team that there was no going back, Deco ended up on the bench because I felt that it was also important to show them that no player – no matter how good or how important he was to the team – would play if he wasn't doing well. Deco wasn't playing well at that time, and he had physical and psychological problems. So, in terms of the team, it was important to leave him on the bench even though we weren't winning. When I read some of my players' interviews today, it reinforces my belief that that

15. A Portuguese newspaper.

decision was both right and important. They recognise the fact that I treat them all equally and that I will leave any one of them out, regardless of their importance. I must also say that Deco was a great professional, as he unreservedly accepted my decision as the right one."

Thus, the match against Leiria didn't yield good results, nor was Mourinho well received by the members of União de Leiria.

"I had no problems with the players or the Board. Everybody welcomed me, and many people were happy to see me again. As for the Leiria members, things weren't quite the same. Probably unaware of the money I'd left behind in the club's coffers, but remembering that I'd said I would stay in Leiria until the end of the season, I heard some whistling and jeering when I walked onto the pitch. I am sure that their reaction stemmed, above all, from the admiration they have for me in that city. If they didn't think I was good, they would simply have ignored me."

The final result, 1-1, meant a four-point difference between Porto and Benfica. However, it wasn't all bad news, and there was an increasingly positive view that the 'kids' would bear fruit sooner or later.

"From a tactical point of view, the 'kids' behaved very well. It was the first time I had tried the formation with which we won the UEFA Cup, i.e. a 4-4-2 formation. In terms of the team's tactical organisation, I got an excellent response and I was convinced that it was the ideal formation for certain situations."

> ON TRACK FOR THE UEFA CUP

FC Porto played their next match at home, against Gil Vicente. At half-time, Porto were losing. Five minutes into the second half José Mourinho sent on Cândido Costa, and turned the game around. The 'kid' scored two goals in twenty minutes and Porto won. But the most important part of this round of matches, for the Porto fans too, didn't take place at Antas Stadium, but rather at Benfica's Stadium. In a seemingly easy match, Benfica drew 1-1 with Sporting de Braga. Zahovic scored a goal 71 minutes into the game, as a result of a dubious penalty. By that time the referee had already ignored a clear foul

by a Benfica player in the penalty area which, had it been conceded, would have meant a 2-0 win for Sporting de Braga. This led to another of Mourinho's comments receiving considerable media coverage: *"I hope that it hasn't been set down in stone that Benfica have to be third"*.

The difference in points between the teams dropped from four to two. Thus, with only five matches until the end of the championship, Benfica were in third place with 55 points, and FC Porto in fourth with 53 points.

The next match for both teams was away. Benfica against Santa Clara, in the Azores, and FC Porto against Farense, in Faro.

Before the start of FC Porto's match with Farense, the Benfica match had already ended in a goalless draw. It wasn't difficult to put two and two together. If FC Porto won, they would be level with Benfica, but as Porto were at an advantage in terms of the games both teams had played, Mourinho's team would once again be in third place. Spurred on by Benfica's defeat, Porto went on to win by a resounding 3-0. It was their second consecutive win, and marked their return to the European championship spot in only two games. The team was enjoying a second wind. This match calendar also looked easier than Benfica's. FC Porto were to play Guimarães and Santa Clara at home, and Braga and Paços de Ferreira away. As for Benfica, things looked decidedly more complicated as they would play two away matches against Sporting and Marítimo, and two matches at home to Paços de Ferreira and Boavista.

"I felt that it was our great opportunity to start to work things out, in our favour. Deco made a good comeback, as did Baía and McCarthy, who had been injured. Whereas Benfica had had two draws, we'd enjoyed two wins. This gave us the push we needed and made Benfica shake. Furthermore, to be back in the running for a European position was also incredibly encouraging. Everything was in our favour, and I felt that we couldn't let the opportunity to assert ourselves once and for all slip by. We had to achieve our objectives, which at that moment included reaching third place in the Portuguese League – the place that represented access to the UEFA Cup. However, I still had some doubts. I wasn't totally confident in that group, and I didn't know how this team was going to react now that the pressure was on."

But the team reacted well. After a 3-0 win against Faro, Porto went on to beat Guimarães 3-0, and Braga 4-0. All in all, this totalled four consecutive wins, where they'd scored twelve goals and only conceded one. However, with two matches to go until the end of the season, the question of third place was still up in the air. Benfica beat Paços de Ferreira, and drew 1-1 against Sporting. Now they were only two points away from Porto, and still in the running.

As for Mourinho's 'eleven', the team structure for the following year – or at least most of it – was beginning to take shape: Vítor Baía; Secretário, Ricardo Carvalho, Jorge Andrade and Mário Silva; Paredes, Alenitchev, Deco and Capucho; Hélder Postiga and McCarthy. At the end of the season, Jorge Andrade, Paredes and McCarthy left – but only for financial reasons, not because Mourinho wanted to see them go. Others came.

> JOSÉ MOURINHO'S 'BIBLE'

It was around this time that José Mourinho handed the famous 'Bible' to Jorge Nuno Pinto da Costa.

"I think this type of document is extremely important because it guides and directs an entire process. This document is a PowerPoint presentation that I gave to the president. The very first diagram sets out the idea that is the basis for the whole programme: 'The concept of club is more important than any player'. This concept is presented by itself on the first slide and is the basis for the entire structure of the document. It is a belief that must be taken on by everyone in the club, especially the junior ranks.

I wanted everyone in FC Porto always to be aware that what is important in terms of a game philosophy, when we think, speak and practise football, is that the game's principles are much more important than what each player thinks in relation to that very same game. The way the team organises a match is the most important factor of all. Furthermore, respect for the club, for its norms, for its philosophy, etc, is much more important than any individual. The document I drew up, and which some now refer to as the 'Bible', is totally in line with this principle. Also, the stand taken by the president, Pinto da Costa, had been a great help in terms of having these ideas adhered to in the club. I think that he was the first to think this way, i.e. that no one comes before the club. Here is a man who has the club at his feet, with thousands of people saying that the new stadium should bear his name. However, he rejects that idea because he feels that the symbolism of the Dragon[16] *should always be present. I think that this says it all with regard to his character and the way he views and runs the club.*

Pinto da Costa is the first to think that no one comes before the club

In relation to the practical aspects of a football team, I held to the following principles, among others: Portuguese players on the team, or if you like 'to Portuguesify' the squad; to work towards a lower average of players; objective-based contracts; signing players from lower teams whose

16. FC Porto's new stadium has been renamed and is now "Stadium of the Dragon".

professionals earn less, but with great rewards should they win; title-based targets and targets based on playing time."

In the penultimate match before the end of the season, FC Porto were at home to Santa Clara, in what could prove to be a decisive match if Benfica failed to beat Boavista. However, Santa Clara arrived at Antas Stadium hell-bent on winning.

"I cannot vouch for it, but I heard that Santa Clara had been offered a 'monumental' match bonus. I even heard that they would receive a lump sum greater than any player's monthly salary. The truth of the matter is that they went to Antas to play the match of their lives, and by the end of the first 45 minutes they were winning 2-1, which meant we'd lose third place. At half-time I gave my shortest-ever talk as FC Porto's coach. 'Be calm, we're playing well. Carry on playing this way because we are going to win.'

It ended up being an electrifying match. My team played an excellent second half and we won 5-3. We had almost accomplished our mission."

Going into their final match, FC Porto were also fighting for a place in the Champions League. In order to do so, they had to beat Paços de Ferreira, and hope that Boavista wouldn't beat Vitória de Setúbal at Bessa Stadium. Porto went on to win, but back at Bessa Stadium things got complicated and Vitória lost. In this way, FC Porto were assured of their third place and subsequently qualified for the 2002/2003 UEFA Cup.

In the meantime, however, the groundwork had already been laid for the next season. Only the problems with the left wing needed solving; another wide-playing midfielder was necessary, as was another forward. And so, Mourinho was counting on: Vítor Baía, Paulo Santos and Hilário; Paulo Ferreira and Secretário; Nuno Valente and Mário Silva; Jorge Costa and Jorge Andrade; Ricardo Carvalho and Pedro Emanuel; Costinha, Paredes and Paulinho Santos; Maniche and Alenitchev; Deco and Bruno; Capucho and Cândido Costa; Clayton and someone who was still to come; Hélder Postiga and another striker; and finally Derlei, the coach's trump card. This is how the season had been planned, with two players for each position, and only two vacancies.

Even before Mourinho went on holiday, Jorge Nuno Pinto da Costa managed to take advantage of an opportunity which had arisen. Benfica were interested in keeping Jankauskas, but only as a loan player. Mourinho liked him, and as the Lithuanian player's former club were only open to selling him, the FC Porto president began negotiations. The sum asked for was considered acceptable, and Jankauskas was signed to add to the squad's group of strikers along with Hélder Postiga. Thus, only one player was missing from the left wing to share the position with Clayton. Mourinho wanted César Peixoto, but the deal hadn't yet been sealed. In the end, César Peixoto would be signed only two days before the beginning of the season.

And so, Mourinho went on holiday, all the while keeping in touch with Antas Stadium.

Three days into the new season, Jorge Andrade left for Deportivo La Coruña, forcing the coach to make further changes. The deal with the Spanish club included the return of Nuno to Portugal, this time to Antas, and to make up for Jorge Andrade's absence, Mourinho called up Ricardo Costa, who until then had been on the B team.

Soon after, Paredes was sold to Regina, in Italy, and José Mourinho asked FC Porto to sign Tiago from União de Leiria.

This was the squad that would kick off the season, and it would only be changed in December upon the arrival of Marco Ferreira and the departure of Hilário and Cândido Costa.

>> CHAPTER V **A CLEAN SWEEP**

FC PORTO 2002/03

MY GROUP
BARRED FROM THE CHANGING ROOMS
THE VÍTOR BAÍA CASE
RESTING WITH THE BALL AND PLAYER ROTATION
THE 'GOOD END' BEGINS
THE FIRST DEFEAT
A HUGE DISAPPOINTMENT
THE BEST MATCH OF THE SEASON
THE FIRST TITLE
THE FINAL AT SEVILLE
THE PORTUGUESE CUP

>> CHAPTER V **A CLEAN SWEEP**

And so the 2002/03 season began. A glorious season, considered at the time by Jorge Nuno Pinto da Costa to be *"FC Porto's best ever"*. Nobody knew, or foresaw it, at the start of the season. José Mourinho was aware that he had a promise to keep, but he wasn't overly concerned. The club hadn't won the Portuguese League for three years, something unheard-of in the previous 20 years of the club's history. The members were after titles and José Mourinho felt ready to take on the greatest challenge of his career. For only the second time, he was starting a season with a squad of his choice, and for the first time he hoped to see the season through.

> *MY GROUP*

Within the available budget, Mourinho had the team he'd envisaged. He felt confident of the players he'd chosen, who would allow him to fight for the national title.

"The first working week was very important because the players who'd gone to the World Cup hadn't yet returned, and they represented most of the players who were staying on from the previous season – i.e. those who had played for Porto, and therefore those I already knew. So, during the first week I worked only with the new players. I think they benefited a lot from this. It made it possible for them to enter the group and get into the work methods without any pressure from the more 'important' players. This was positive in relation to the hesitation that new players always experience. Without the 'older' ones around, they were more open and true to themselves, which was very important in terms of my getting to know them well.

Furthermore, with regard to my methodology, I was able to start from scratch with them. It would have been more complicated with the others around. You need only think of an exercise, which is a matter of routine for the 'older' ones and something completely new for those who have just arrived. It's like teaching English to a roomful of students, where some are beginners and others are advanced learners. So, in this specific case, the absence of some benefited others. They managed to grasp my exercises and the vocabulary I generally use.

Then, when the other players arrived we set off for France, for our training period at Saint-Etiénne. At the end of three days' work, I started to get some feedback from the older players. 'Mister, not only are these new guys excellent, they're also great 'kids'.'"

And José Mourinho understood that he was building a solid, cohesive group with a future. This view was further reinforced on the fifth day of training.

"On that day I gave them the afternoon off, as well as the evening. The only thing I asked of them was to be back at the hotel by 11:00 pm. I didn't see them leave, but I began to see them return. I was with my assistants in the hotel lobby, waiting for the players to arrive. Usually, some of them come back late because there are always those players who prefer to pay a fine in order to stay out a little later. I was wrong. It was around twenty to eleven when a taxi arrived with the first group of players. Immediately after this, all the other players began to arrive as well. I was completely taken aback, not only because they'd arrived before the stipulated time, but also because they all arrived at the same time. Jorge Costa walked past me, and I asked him, 'Jorge, what happened?'

'We all went out together. We have a great group here, Mister.'

It's difficult to put into words what a coach feels when he hears the captain say something like this. Over twenty men who'd been together for only five days, had chosen to go out together, have dinner together and hang out with each other on their first afternoon and evening off. It was the birth of my group."

He also decided to carefully analyse the player's moral fibre

And it was indeed the group that José Mourinho had planned for and selected. Now, it wasn't enough to be a good player to join the Porto ranks. Mourinho also decided to carefully analyse the players' character – their moral fibre. Apart from good players, he was also looking for good men. Football is a collective sport and quality must therefore stem from the group as a whole. In order for a team to work, it must be made up of men of character who view the group as more important than any individual by himself. Only the group is important, and it is only the group that is worth preserving.

A sign on the doors to the changing rooms at Porto's Antas stadium reads *'Here, nobody is allowed in... except us!'* The former FC Porto coach believes that this should be respected; and so we enter a new phase, almost a break with the content and style that has been adopted so far. As this is José Mourinho's 'group', all that's left for the coach to do is to close the door, and without revealing too much about what went on in the changing rooms, I will show how José Mourinho led his group to victory; how he coaches and trains his players, what methods he uses and why. We'll take a look at his choices, his dilemmas and doubts. We'll see how the closed door to the changing rooms – which even now won't be opened – set FC Porto on the path to the 'treble', when in one season they won the Portuguese Super League, the UEFA Cup and the Portuguese Cup. A feat that up until 2003 only 6 teams – and 6 coaches – had managed to achieve in Europe.

During the pre-season training period, José Mourinho did something he had never done before. In every warm-up match, he played the first half with eleven players, and the second half with another set of eleven players. In so doing, Mourinho sought mainly to achieve two objectives: competitiveness amongst the players, and a greater spirit of solidarity and friendship. Those who played during the first half were sent back to the bench with the 'obligation' to give tips to their substitutes, who in turn had previously supported the first-half players. He got the results he was after, and was increasingly confident of the 'group' he was building. A friendly, strong, cohesive and determined group.

"The end of the warm-up match against Paris Saint Germain was very strange. We had to go to penalties, and during the second set I was thinking

about who should go on to score, when Maniche – looking very decisive – suddenly told me, 'Mister, I'll go and score now.'

I looked at him in utter disbelief and replied, 'But you went off at half-time, you can't take a penalty now.'

'Let me go; the guy doesn't see, he won't even notice.'

He tightened the laces on his boots, and completely unperturbed and without looking back once, he went off to score the penalty. I watched incredulously as he walked up to the penalty mark, adjusted the ball, took a few steps back, ran and scored. After that, Hilário saved the next penalty and we won the Cup. Without being able to, Maniche had scored the penalty that led to victory."

For the first time since arriving at FC Porto he decided to change tactics and play with a 4x4x2 formation

FC Porto's pre-season unfolded calmly, as work was carried out steadily and in a spirit of harmony. As for targets, Mourinho increasingly believed that they should strive towards winning the Portuguese League. The Portuguese Cup could be theirs or not, depending on the luck of the draw, as well as the position that they would find themselves in as the championship went on, which might make it more difficult to work towards other competitions. As for the UEFA Cup, the target was for the club to carry out its best-ever campaign – to make it to the semi-finals. This was José Mourinho's secret ambition.

The first League match didn't go well. FC Porto were at home to Belenenses and 'managed' to draw 2-2.

"It didn't come as a surprise to me. Deco and Alenitchev had to sit out that match, so there was no one to coordinate the midfield/attack link. It was the first match of the season, with all the pressure and responsibility this entails, and we were up against an opponent that created an atmosphere of tension, as they were traditionally hard to beat. It was all very uneasy. The pre-season had been prepared with Deco and Alenitchev in mind, without taking into account that they wouldn't be able to play the opening match. During the week, we tried different strategies, I had a great many doubts and everything was very difficult.

As for the game itself, I feel that there was none to speak of. Belenenses went out with the sole purpose of upsetting and destabilising FC Porto. There was no game. It was all about holding up the match, freezing the ball, simulated fouls, simulated injuries, stretcher-bearers coming onto the field, the referee being carried away by this unfair play, my team getting worked up, etc, etc, etc.

So, for all these reasons I was not surprised we drew against Belenenses. But I must confess that I was bothered by the fact that we hadn't won, unlike Benfica and Sporting, who had both won their opening matches of the season."

> BARRED FROM THE CHANGING ROOMS

Mourinho didn't waste any time. That very day, immediately after the match, he met with the rest of the coaching staff and started to prepare for the next game against Boavista. There and then, a new strategy was planned. José Mourinho decided to change tactics and to play with a 4-4-2 formation.

"I felt that Boavista played a very direct game. The game was basically built around Ricardo and the two strikers, and I wanted Costinha to be the fixed player in front of the midfielders. With this positioning, and speaking in aerial terms, I wanted Costinha to be able 'to clean up' all situations so that my midfielders wouldn't be first-ball men, but rather second-ball men – or if you like deflection men. In this way, we could calmly cancel out any of their offensive initiatives. The truth of the matter is that from this point on, by always gaining the second ball as we did, there was never any danger of a goal being scored against us during the match."

However, we should not assume that a lack of dangerous moves on the pitch corresponded to a lack of danger at Bessa Stadium. José Mourinho watched the match from a box as he had been banned from the Belenenses game.

"What happened at half-time at Bessa was something we had foreseen and so we were ready for it. They wouldn't let me into the changing rooms to speak to my players. Unlike UEFA games, in the Super League a coach who is banned from the bench can speak to his players at half-time. So, when the referee blew the whistle at the end of the first half, I headed for the lift to the changing

rooms. Suddenly, João Loureiro, the Boavista president, ran past me and stepped into the lift. The door closed. I waited patiently for the lift to come back, until I realised that it wasn't moving. I thought it might have broken down or something and headed for the stairs. A Boavista security guard was standing at the door to the stairs and wouldn't let me through, saying that no one was allowed past there.

As I know Portuguese football well and because, as I said, I'd foreseen the situation, we took a 'loud speaker' phone into the changing rooms. I returned to the box, sat down, made a call and finally got to speak to my players. I started off with a joke. 'I'm stuffed. You're beating Boavista 1-0, Brito is twisting the knife, and I'll be unemployed after this game'. The players immediately started laughing and shouting, 'Brito is the greatest!'

After this bit of banter, I became more serious and warned them to keep their emotions under control as Boavista were putting a lot of pressure on the player with the ball. It was important for them to move the ball out of the pressure area with lots of cross-field passes so that the other team couldn't pressurise a specific target, and finally I told them to win the match.

André, Dr. Fernando Gomes and I were literally kicked out of the stadium

At the end, there was trouble again. André, Dr Fernando Gomes and I were literally kicked out of the stadium. We thought we'd wait in the box for everyone to leave, so that we could then go down to the changing rooms. Once again, we were not allowed to go down by lift, nor could we stay in the box. Together with the other spectators who'd watched the match in the same place, we were led to the exit. Suddenly, we were outside, surrounded by Boavista fans. We made a dash for the hotel, which was near the stadium, and, in this way, surprised the crowd who looked amazed but did not react to our being there. Nevertheless, as we ran, the sentence I heard the most was, 'There goes that son-of-a-b… Mourinho.'"

As for the game, not only was this their first win in the championship, but Nuno also made his debut as FC Porto's goalkeeper. Vítor Baía had injured his eye during the week, and was not considered fit to play by Porto's clinical department. And so, Nuno played his first match without conceding any goals, and with a 1-0 win.

This was followed by a 3-1 win at home against Gil Vicente, and for the fourth match Porto once again had a difficult away game, this time against Vitória de Guimarães. FC Porto won 2-0, and today Mourinho has no doubts that the first two consecutive wins away were decisive and had a positive impact on the rest of the League season for Porto.

"In the previous championship, FC Porto had won no points in the two corresponding matches. Also, we'd started this championship badly by drawing with Belenenses, and if any or both of these games had gone badly, we would have been in a very uncomfortable position in the table. Benfica and Sporting would have had a dramatic lead, not necessarily in terms of points, but certainly at the psychological level.

We didn't play brilliantly in these two games – as we did in some others – nor did we dominate. Nevertheless, we won convincingly and played solidly. We reacted well to a good Boavista and a good Guimarães, and this spurred us on for the rest of the championship. In terms of away games, this was the best tonic for a team that had suffered many defeats away in the previous season – in Alvalade, Guimarães, Bessa, Aveiro, the Azores, Paços de Ferreira, Belém, etc."

> THE VÍTOR BAÍA CASE

In between the Gil Vicente and Vitória de Guimarães matches, FC Porto made their UEFA Cup debut. At home to Polonia Warszawa, they won 6-0, a result that immediately laid to rest any doubts about them having been lucky during the knockout round. After the match, Vítor Baía, who was still reserve goalkeeper as Nuno was playing well, gave an interview to *Record*, on 22 September. It would become the basis for a misunderstanding between Mourinho and himself, as well as the main topic of conversation in the Portuguese sports world for several weeks. In the interview, Baía expressed his dissatisfaction at being a reserve to Nuno.

"That wasn't the main issue, though. It should be noted that FC Porto had broken off all ties with the newspaper Vítor gave the interview to. It was therefore against the rules for any Porto professional, myself included, to give

Record an interview. So, whether we agreed with this or not, as employees on the club's payroll we could not 'speak' to Record. As he had broken this rule, I had to confront him in the changing rooms about the interview, telling him that he shouldn't have given it and that he'd have to notify the Board officially of what had happened. Regretting this fact, I told him that's what he'd have to do.

Vítor disagreed, saying that he hadn't given them the interview directly. According to him, everything the paper had printed was no more than a conversation he'd had with several journalists, where the latter had in fact asked him some questions, which he'd answered. Then everything appeared in writing in the Record. Even so, I told him that we'd still have to go ahead with the disciplinary process, all the while guaranteeing him that when he came back, he'd be on an equal footing with all the others when it came to fighting for a place in the team. I gave the same guarantees to the team's captain. I told Jorge Costa that I always played with those who are the fittest, and that I don't need to be friendly or on good terms with a player in order to put him on the pitch. So they didn't need to worry about the future of their team-mate. When the suspension ended, he would work and have the same opportunities as everyone else."

Once the report drawn up by José Mourinho had been handed to the FC Porto/SAD Board, things followed their due course, and were no longer in the coach's hands. In the meantime, Vitor Baía was suspended until the enquiry was over. During the training session for the match against Guimarães, the president, Pinto da Costa, spoke to the rest of the squad. He told the players that the disciplinary process was underway and repeated what Mourinho had already said about Baía's future. He also took the opportunity to announce that FC Porto had extended José Mourinho's contract for another year.

"I viewed the situation as a reinforcement of the President's confidence in the coach and that nothing, and no-one, would shake that confidence. On the other hand, I believe that this shows how the president Pinto da Costa feels about football and everything surrounding it."

And so FC Porto continued on its path with Vitor Baía working on the sidelines. After the match against Guimarães, the keeper apologised to Mourinho and to his team-mates, a *mea culpa* that moved everyone in the Porto changing rooms. However, the process had already started and had to run its course.

The next match against Marítimo at Antas Stadium saw Porto win 2-0. An away match in Aveiro against Beira-Mar followed, and their second draw at 1-1.

It wasn't the best of results, especially before the difficult match against Benfica that lay ahead. First place in the Super League was at stake. Preparation for this game wasn't carried out in the best way, as the National Team had played three international games the week before. The Porto players on the Portugal team only arrived at Antas Stadium on the Thursday, that is, three days before the match. The game was marred by Jorge Costa being sent off 30 minutes into the match for allegedly striking Simão Sabrosa. This forced José Mourinho to adopt a plan they had previously practised.

At half-time I told them that the Benfica players were 'shit-scared'

He knew that sooner or later he would be faced with a situation where he'd have ten of his players up against his opponent's eleven players. Mourinho likes to foresee everything so that nothing is left to chance. Thus, on several occasions he had practised a flexible 4-3-2 formation. Mourinho feels that even when a team is at a disadvantage, it doesn't necessarily have to lose its attacking power and can go in search of a win, even if it is one player short. Many practices were held with ten players versus eleven, in order for players to adapt to the situation. The first great test of this plan was against Benfica, when they were forced to put this formation into practice and reap the benefits of their very specific training.

"The team reacted automatically and adapted incredibly well to the numerical disadvantage. The midfielders and the two players in front, although outnumbered, immediately knew how to keep up the pressure, and

in objective terms, they acted as if they had an equal number of players. Usually when teams are one player short, they immediately change their playing philosophy, and if the score is level they stop thinking about winning. That wasn't the case with us."

The match was tied 1-1 when Jorge Costa was sent off. When the game was over FC Porto had won 2-1. Nevertheless, the coach didn't stop here.

"I think that if there were matches where my work and participation were decisive, then the game against Benfica was one of them. At half-time we were tied 1-1, and we were playing with ten men. Under those circumstances, a draw wouldn't even have been a bad result, as we would hold onto first place in the Super League without conceding any points to our direct rivals, Benfica. At half-time I told them that the Benfica players were 'shit scared', and that even with an extra player they wouldn't take us on. They'd wait, possibly expecting us to make a mistake, and try to beat us as we got more tired as a result of being a player short. In short, they'd do everything except 'hound' us.

That's when I played my last card. I continued speaking to my players and told them that since they wouldn't take us on, we'd have to take them on. I told them to push Benfica up against 'a brick wall', and to dominate the match. If we did that, we would win for sure. We won and it was very important to have done so under those circumstances and with the superiority we displayed."

And, with the exception of the goalkeeper Nuno, who would be replaced by Vítor Baía, this was the team that Mourinho would use most often during the entire season: Nuno; Paulo Ferreira, Jorge Costa, Pedro Emanuel and Nuno Valente; Costinha, Deco and Maniche; Capucho, Postiga and Derlei.

After the match against Benfica, Vítor Baía went back to work. FC Porto were soon to play União de Leiria in Marinha Grande. Once again, this game ended in a draw, 2-2, with Nuno having his worst performance.

"Three days later we were scheduled to play the second knock-out round in the UEFA Cup against Austria Vienna. If it hadn't been for this game, I would probably have given Nuno time to steady himself and to recover emotionally in order to continue as goalkeeper. But the match against Austria was just around the corner. I spoke with the rest of my coaching staff on the way back to Oporto from Marinha Grande, and I clearly remember André

asking what type of approach I was thinking of using in Austria."

I immediately replied, 'We're going with the intention of sorting out the match there and then. I don't like to leave a qualifying round to be sorted out in the second leg during a home match.'

'From an attacking point of view, I would feel more comfortable with Vítor as goalkeeper if I were playing. Who knows if this unfortunate spell for Nuno isn't the ideal time to change keeper?' said André.

I still spoke with Silvino as Vítor had only been training with us for a week, but my goalkeeper coach immediately set my mind at ease. 'Vítor has had a week of training like no other. He's extremely motivated and has no physical limitations, so he is completely fit to play whenever you wish.' In light of the above information, I decided to replace Nuno with Vítor in Vienna, where we went on to win 1-0."

FC Porto put on an excellent performance, which prompted Pinto da Costa to say *"This team is as good as the one from Vienna,"* a reference to the historic team that had become European champions there in a match against Bayern Munich.

On 4 November, FC Porto beat Nacional da Madeira in a home match which should have been straightforward but wasn't. The team was tired and worn out as a result of that week's fantastic European match, though its opponents were theoretically weaker as they had just moved up a division. Everything was set for the players to make it easy for the other team at the slightest hint of carelessness. In fact, FC Porto were losing 1-0 at one stage, but in an impressive show of professionalism and willpower the players managed to turn things round, and once again FC Porto won, 5-1. This game started a cycle of 13 consecutive wins.

> RESTING WITH THE BALL & PLAYER ROTATION

FC Porto were already practically a team in the image of José Mourinho. Certain characteristics stemming from the philosophy of their coach were beginning to appear in all their splendour. The players had basically assimilated all the ideas and FC Porto were now at their peak.

"It was at this time that we began to accentuate our pressure as a fundamental characteristic of the team's way of playing. It was in the match against Nacional da Madeira that the team carried out the most perfect pressing, up until that point. So much so that Nacional's coach, José Peseiro, told me the following week that his players had never ended a match feeling as tired as they did after playing us."

However, it's not only the opponents who have to run. By chasing the ball and stepping up the pressure, FC Porto also had to run a great deal. That is where the second part of José Mourinho's specific training comes in. Aware that physically it is difficult for the players to keep pressure on all the time, it is necessary for them to be able to rest on the field.

"It's what I call 'resting with the ball'. With the pace of play that we impose, it's necessary to rest; otherwise no one will make it to the end of the match. The best way to do this, and run fewer risks, is to rest when we have the ball.

In the game against Nacional, we managed to do this in a rather effective, almost perfect, way. Basically, it's about alternating moments of great intensity and pressure with periods of rest with the ball, which is nothing more than gaining ball possession but with the intention of resting. It's possession for possession's sake, with no sporting objective. I have the ball at my feet, I have the game under control and I don't run, thus allowing me to rest."

In the two weeks that were to follow, FC Porto would play both matches away. In between, they'd also play Austria Vienna, which at the outset wasn't to prove too difficult.

As for the matches for the Portuguese League, the first was in Setúbal, where Porto won 1-0. It was a game that José Mourinho felt and admitted they might not have won.

"It was a very difficult match. Our opponents were strong, and in terms of the game itself, or as a result of an error on the referee's part when he

disallowed a goal by Vitória de Setúbal, the score could have gone the other way."

The match against Moreirense was an entirely different story and the blue-and-white team won convincingly.

Later, on 28 November, there was the FC Porto/Lens match. Once again, fate didn't smile upon Mourinho's pupils, who had to face an opponent from the Champions League, who had only been ousted by 'giants' such as Deportivo da Coruña, AC Milan (who went on to win the competition), and Bayern Munich. Lens, ranked second in the French League, had lost their away matches in Coruña and Milan, and drawn in Munich. In terms of home matches, they had managed two wins and a draw.

It wasn't an easy task, but it wasn't impossible either. The French goalkeeper played a key role in the first home match, and two 'give aways' helped the score to 3-0. And so began the UEFA Cup dream. Practically guaranteed moving on to the next round, FC Porto would continue to be in the competition for at least a few more months as it would only start up again towards the end of February 2003, with the quarter-finals. This left them enough time to manage the squad, study their opponents and try to win the Portuguese League – the main objective of the season. Furthermore, FC Porto could continue to say that it was active on all fronts, something that has always provided an excellent incentive for players.

From a defensive point of view 'offensive pressing' on the opposing goal

José Mourinho's game plan was fully assimilated and put into practice.

"From a defensive point of view, as much pressure as possible, or as we say technically, 'offensive pressing' on the opposing goal. Very close lines, with particular emphasis on the defensive line, which must be very close to the midfield line so that the forwards can put pressure on the opponent's defence. This means that the defenders must have a natural formation in order to play with 40 metres of open space behind them.

In the midfield, a very well defined triangle, where the player Deco had the most freedom in terms of moving from his position, as the attacking formation focused on ball possession – I'd even say it focused on excessive ball possession time. With this characteristic – which our team had already acquired by this time and which became its distinguishing feature – we went in search of ball movement. But it was ball movement for ball movement's sake, without a particular objective, so that we could then introduce other game elements aimed at going further, consequently creating dangerous and potential goal situations.

In this regard, training was always intense. We practised specific situations in order to know at any moment whether we should take a risk and attack as soon as we got the ball, or whether we should keep the ball moving because it didn't seem as if the conditions were there to create danger.

All of this because, as we have seen, the way my team plays is very draining. When we don't have the ball, we immediately start looking for ways to regain it, even if it means going into the opponent's area. This wears the players out, and so once they've regained the ball they have to decide if they can attack successfully and continue to wear themselves out, or if, on the contrary, they cannot and must choose to rest and keep the ball moving.

By this stage in the Portuguese League, my team knew perfectly well what to decide, and Costinha was a key player in this plan as he always chose wisely. So, when people said that we were always in better physical shape than the others, or even that our preparation was different, I was always quick to say that that wasn't it. It was really about our ability to manage the game; we rested more than the others.

This fact alone made it possible for us to go on looking apparently as fresh as ever after 50 matches. All in all, it is our concept – Rui Faria's and mine – that the 'physical side' alone doesn't exist. For us, to say that this or that player is in great physical shape is a mistake. The player is either fit or not. And what do we mean by being fit? It is to be physically well and to be part of a game plan, which a player knows inside out. With regard to the psychological side, which is essential to play at the highest level, a fit player feels confident, cooperates with and believes in his team-mates, and shows solidarity towards them. All of this put together means a player is fit and it is reflected in playing well."

FC Porto were indeed fit and so the team continued their winning streak.

It was at this point that José Mourinho started to implement a squad rotation system. Between the Super League, the UEFA Cup and the National

Team, FC Porto played five matches in the second fortnight of November. No-one can cope with so many consecutive games and so it was necessary to study how to manage the squad right down to the very last detail.

"In fact, we started using player rotation in a Portuguese Cup match against Trofense. I remember that many people had some doubts about that game. Is he really going to opt for player rotation or has he changed the team simply because the opponent is from a lower division?

I felt that without squad rotation we wouldn't be able to continue being successful

I feel all doubts were cleared up. In that set of matches, there was significant squad rotation. For example, those who played against Moreirense and in the National Team didn't play in the game against Trofense. Then, most of the players who played at home against Lens didn't play at Antas against Académica.

This is when the rotation system began, with extremely positive practical results: we continued winning and we kept up with our coherent play. Thus, this rotation was absolutely decisive in terms of the 'treble' we managed to achieve that season. It's impossible for a human being to play the number of games we did during the season – and there were over 50 – and to do so at the pace we did. There must be intervals in which to rest."

It was at this time, between the matches against Académica and Santa Clara (both of which FC Porto won) that Mourinho also ran into his first problem with the Portuguese League. The coach's statement in the newspapers was crushing: *"They thought we wouldn't make it"*. This was Mourinho's reply to the match calendar established by the League. Santa Clara were a match behind, against Marítimo. This game, set by the League, made it impossible to reschedule the match against FC Porto, just at a time the Porto players were getting ready to play their second leg game against Lens in the 3rd qualifying round of the UEFA Cup.

As is common in these circumstances, the Super League match could not be brought forward and had to be played on Sunday, 8 December, at 7:00 pm, while the game against Lens was to be held in France, on 12 December. As expected, FC Porto made it to the next round, which would only be played on

20 February. This gave José Mourinho the time he needed to dedicate himself, almost exclusively, to the main Portuguese competition.

The next game was at home to Paços de Ferreira; and after all the antics that had taken place previously, it allowed José Mourinho to draw one of the most important conclusions of the entire season.

"This match was vitally important because it left me in no doubt as to my rotation theory. The game against Paços de Ferreira turned out to be the one we came the closest to losing, but ended up winning. We had practically played two games in a row, without changing players in the team. Also we'd had two exhausting trips one after the other – to the Azores and France.

It was at this point that I felt the team wasn't able to play its game. We won 2-1 in the last minute, when moments before Vítor Baía had made a great save. So, we might perfectly well have lost that match. At that moment, I clearly felt that without squad rotation we wouldn't be able to continue being as successful as we'd been in the three different competitions. Whereas before, player rotation had been a question of management, from this point on it became a question of necessity. So, we started using it much more regularly."

It was practically the end of the year, but before that FC Porto still made their way to Póvoa where they beat Varzim 2-0. It was their third consecutive win away, without conceding a single goal.

Seven points ahead of the team in second place in the League, they were in a comfortable position, as well as still being in the running for the UEFA Cup and the Portuguese Cup. José Mourinho didn't ask Santa Claus for anything special. He was quite happy with what he had, and meant to hold onto it;

especially because Christmas, with the changes it brings, is so often a turning point for teams. Many teams manage to improve when they're not doing well, but the reverse is also true for those that are doing well.

As far as José Mourinho was concerned, everything could continue just as it was. Only one thing changed – and that came in the form of a gift from Pinto da Costa. Yielding to the coach's wishes, the FC Porto president went to Setúbal to get Vitória's main star. Marco Ferreira was signed.

> THE 'GOOD END' BEGINS

When in Setúbal, José Mourinho has chosen to live in a magnificent duplex, right in the city centre. All he has to do is cross the street and he's in the Bonfim Park, the oldest and best-known green space in the city. Mourinho has spent many an hour there with his children, on the swings, the slides and the green lawns that cover most of the park. Right next door, there is the stadium, which bears the same name.

Thirty-five years before, instead of heading towards the park's lawns, little Zé Mário would go with his father to the green grass of the stadium. Mourinho Félix trained as goalkeeper for Vitória de Setúbal, and his ever-attentive son would fetch all the balls that didn't make their way to the goal. Back then, as now, everything related to the Bonfim Stadium in one way or another. Bonfim (The Good End) was the motto for the 2002/2003 season.

In Porto, José Mourinho began to see the 'good end' right at the beginning of the year, which brought with it two matches in Lisbon. Two consecutive away games at the Restelo and Alvalade stadiums led Mourinho to reason as follows: *"It is the most important stage of all in the Super League. If we get four points we'll continue to control our destiny, which is essential to our success. If we get fewer points, things might get complicated."*

The seven-point lead might not prove enough in case of defeat. Furthermore, FC Porto had lost at both the Restelo and Alvalade stadiums the previous season. At that point, Sporting were still in contention for the Portuguese title and Belenenses were trying to make it to the European competition. There was only one certainty: they were facing two difficult matches.

"In between these two games, we still had a match at Antas against Gil Vicente in the Portuguese Cup. I staked everything on the squad rotation system. Everything. For the match against Sporting, and the one against Belenenses, I chose to place the best team on the pitch, with the best and the most rested players. We had two trips to Lisbon over a short space of time. That's why we used a completely different team for the match against Gil Vicente.

Apart from the goalkeeper, the only two players who had played against Sporting were Paulo Ferreira and Pedro Emanuel. It was complete player rotation."

'You've got Derlei on my back the whole time; tell the guy to go and play on the other side'

As for results, there were more wins for the blue-and-white team. The first was at Alvalade, a match that drew the attention of the journalists because Mourinho came onto the field and sat on the bench for a long time before the players and referees made their way onto the pitch. We were left with a picture, reproduced in many newspapers, of a pensive coach, looking out at what lay beyond – waiting for the great test. Contrary to much of what was said and written, this wasn't a premeditated act.

"Not at all. As a rule, I usually go on first, and for the match at Alvalade I might have gone on too early without realising it. It happened by chance, especially since we felt that the team was so strong and mature that I had little to convey to them in the changing rooms. However, I did tell them that I wouldn't accept a draw. Then I asked them, 'And what about you? Will you accept a draw, or not?' Practically in unison, the Porto players replied, 'No!' I asked them again, just to make sure there weren't any doubts. 'Think carefully. One little point in the bag, and we're all on our way home. Who'd accept this?'

Once again their reply was negative. 'No, Mister. We want to play and we want to win.'"

They played and won 1-0. The score could have been higher as they completely dominated Sporting throughout most of the game. At the end, Pinto da Costa confessed to Mourinho that in twenty one years as club president he had never seen a team of his play and dominate at Alvalade as they did on that day, 21 January 2003.

Their supremacy was so great, that during the match there was even room for some light-hearted banter between José Mourinho and Sporting's Sá Pinto. The two men knew each other on both professional and personal levels. But there was also another relationship binding them at that time – tenant and landlord – as José Mourinho was living in a house in Oporto owned by Sá Pinto. They have known each other for a long time, and so even when they're opponents they always find the time to exchange a few words or to fool around a little.

"Sá had just come back after an injury that had kept him out of football for a long time, so he could never have been in the best physical shape. Furthermore, he was unlucky as Quiroga, a right back playing right there by my bench, hurt himself soon after he'd gone on. So, Sá had to take on the position of the Argentine player, towards the end of the first half.

At half-time I told my players to put some pressure on Sá Pinto for two reasons. Firstly, he wasn't and had never been a right back, and secondly he couldn't be in great shape, as he hadn't played for a long time. Derlei didn't waste any time and was always on top of Sá for the first 15 minutes of the second half. Everyone knows that Sá is a brave and courageous player who never shies away from a battle, and so he didn't give in to Derlei's attack, always trying not to give him any room to manoeuvre. He fought like a real 'lion'. [17] *However, after a while, I began to feel that he was getting weaker. At one point he ran past me as he went to get a ball that had gone out, and I took the opportunity to call him. 'Sá, come here quickly.'*

'What?' he said, gasping like someone under considerable strain.

'Listen here, are you tired?'

'No kidding. You've got Derlei on my back the whole time; tell the guy to go and play on the other side.'

To which I replied somewhat meanly, 'Then get ready, because a few minutes from now Clayton's going on, full of energy.'

It seems I can still see Sá Pinto's face as he looked at me and said, 'Don't

17. *The lion is the symbol of Sporting.*

do this to me, man. You want to ruin me, you want to finish me off.'

'I don't want to finish you off, I want to finish the game,' I said still laughing."

The match didn't finish as Mourinho had wished as Porto weren't able to score another goal, but it ended with a win for them nonetheless. In practical terms, this meant that Sporting were now 13 points behind FC Porto and definitely out of the running for first place in the League. At the same time, Benfica won another 2 points in a draw against Guimarães. The match at Alvalade was also decisive in terms of public opinion, as it dispelled any doubts, even among the more sceptical, as to the quality of the team. From that moment on, FC Porto were seen as the team most likely to win the League.

The two matches away had started off in the best way, but Porto still had to play Belenenses on 21 January. It was on that day, first thing in the morning, that José Mourinho met the National Team Coach, Luís Felipe Scolari. The Brazilian coach made his way to Hotel Altis, where the team were staying, and there they spoke for several hours. Mourinho didn't even accompany the team on their usual morning outing.

"We basically talked about my players. Scolari wanted to know everything about them, and I was at his entire disposal to answer all his questions and doubts. I'd almost say that we analysed each man, from his height right down to his characteristics. We also touched on the Deco 'case'[18] *and he told me that he was completely in favour of having the player in the Portuguese team.*

This was the first and last time I spoke to him. At the time he asked me if it would be OK to sit in on one or two of our practices and to speak a little more with me. Once again I told him I was at his disposal, but he never sought me out thereafter, and so we never met up again.

However, I must say that I enjoyed speaking to him a great deal. He was

18. At that time Deco, a Brazilian player, was still trying to be naturalised in Portugal.

extremely friendly and open. At the time I thought there'd be a lot of understanding and collaboration between us."

And in this way, the game against Belenenses drew closer and closer. The match was to start at 8:15 pm, and by that time Porto knew that Benfica had won their game in Madeira, which increased the pressure on the team led by José Mourinho.

The match didn't start off well. Belenenses scored first, and at half-time the team from Belém were ahead 1-0. In the changing rooms, Jorge Costa once again showed his mettle as FC Porto's captain.

"What really had a great impact during half-time, apart from all the tactical information I gave my players, was Jorge Costa's speech after I'd left the changing rooms. He turned round and loudly told his fellow players that if they lost the match, he would never – and obviously he wouldn't follow through on this – play football again. He then went on to tell them, with an unswayable conviction, that they'd have to take control of the match and play 'à la Porto', and that if that happened they would leave Belém with another win under their belts. This show of leadership and faith on the part of my captain was exactly what the players needed in order to go out and play a great second half and win the match.

Then, I think it was a fantastic reward for all the work he'd put into the group that in ten minutes Jorge Costa scored the two goals that turned the score around and led us to victory. He deserved this prize more than anyone else."

Thus FC Porto made it through the two matches away in Lisbon unscathed. For the first time they were one step away from the League title thanks to these two wins. Benfica, in second place, were 13 points behind. All the other teams were no longer in the running for first place.

"For me, this was the decisive stage in winning the League. At the very least, it was important that we kept the same number of points between us and the team in second place. In fact, we categorically increased the distance between them and us.

In psychological terms, my players were convinced – once and for all – that the player rotation policy was bang on. Some of them still had some doubts in this regard, and those who had a closer relationship with the assistants would sometimes let on that they thought they didn't need to be substituted and that they could keep up with all the games. This moment dispelled their doubts, and at the same time it reinforced their team spirit and their motivation to practise more, and harder.

They finally all understood that playing today didn't necessarily mean they'd play tomorrow. On the contrary, playing today might mean you weren't called up tomorrow. They began to view all these situations as absolutely normal."

The next match was however somewhat unusual. Fit, and with morale riding high, FC Porto were to meet their rivals, Boavista, after two friendly matches for the National Portuguese Team.

José Mourinho's team won 1-0, with Jankauskas coming on towards the end to resolve the match.

"It was one of those matches that leaves football lovers with a feeling of frustration. There was no great show of football, it was depressing. There were many interruptions and fouls, which turned it into an ugly game. Boavista didn't go to Antas with the intention of playing football, or of letting anyone else play either. We weren't able to overcome this situation, and we played what I feel was our worst game that season. The only good thing to come out of it was the score; that's it."

Boavista didn't go to Antas with the intention of playing football, or of letting anyone else play

This was to be followed by another three wins: in Guimarães for the Portuguese Cup; in Barcelos against Gil Vicente (5-3); and once again against Guimarães, but at Antas this time round, in the League (2-1).

> THE FIRST DEFEAT

There was another match for the National Team, Italy-Portugal, which was set for 12 February. For José Mourinho, the main problem with this was the date, as his team were to play Marítimo in Madeira in a Super League match only three days later. The match had been brought forward from Sunday to Saturday, as Porto would be travelling to Turkey the following Thursday to play Denislizpor in a second leg game in the fourth round of the UEFA Cup. Effectively, this meant that between 11 and 20 February – in only nine days – most of José Mourinho's players would play in three major matches, with all the strenuous physical exertion that implies.

"I brought the match in Madeira forward, thinking that there would be some management of players in the National Team. But I was wrong. Paulo Ferreira, Nuno Valente, etc, all of them were on for the full 90 minutes in Italy. Then they came into Lisbon on a charter flight, arrived at 5 or 6 in the morning, drove up to Oporto and arrived there on Thursday morning. On Friday they travelled to Madeira to play that Saturday. This is what was happening when we faced our first defeat in the League."

However, José Mourinho doesn't attribute the loss in Madeira against Marítimo, the first in the Super League, to this situation.

"Basically, we were short of a little luck, as well as the effectiveness we'd displayed in the other matches. In terms of statistics, the game against Marítimo was the one where we had the greatest number of shots on the opponent's goal in the whole championship. On the other hand, I felt we lost because we thought we could win. We basically wanted to repeat what had happened at Belém, but this time things worked out differently. Marítimo started off by leading, then we managed to draw and were immediately on top of them, looking for a second goal. By that time both sides were playing with 10 players, as Deco and one of their players had been sent off. This created more open spaces, which I thought would work in our favour. However, it was our opponents who scored in a counter-attacking move with 15 minutes to go. We weren't able to reverse this situation and so we faced our first defeat.

At the end, I greeted each of my players individually and told them clearly that no one is unbeatable, and that we had to lose sooner or later. I also told

them that this was a great test as to how the team would react to its first loss – a test that could only be reacted to in a positive way. I asked them to view this defeat as something that was natural, because this is how things are in football.

We went out for dinner that night and although the team was sad, the players were by no means defeated or despondent.

I understood they were unhappy, because nobody likes to lose, but at the same time I wanted them to be calm and to think that we would win the next match. And that is precisely the impression they left me with."

As promised in the previous season, a defeat would always be followed by an open-door practice, and so the next training session at Antas took place in full view of the members. Those who had been expecting disapproval and recriminations were proved wrong. The club members who were present recognised the effort the players had been making, and viewed the loss simply as one of football's possible outcomes. The team were welcomed with open arms and a warm ovation – à la Porto!

Following the defeat in Madeira, there was the match against Denislizpor right in the middle of the week. Not an easy opponent, especially given the way Turkish football had taken off in recent years. In any case, there was the firm conviction that they were a worthy adversary, though the loss against Marítimo did not shake the team's conviction and motivation.

"I've always said that when you win, you can go up to two weeks without playing. However, when you lose, it's best to play the following match the very next day."

Thus, we had the FC Porto – Denislizpor match to make us forget Funchal, Madeira. However, another challenge awaited the group – to beat Silvino, the 'cold foot'. This was yet another 'provocation' on the part of José Mourinho, such was his confidence in the team's recovery and of a favourable result against the Turkish team.

Silvino Louro didn't usually sit on the bench except in European competitions, when another member of the coaching team is allowed. And so, Silvino had been on the bench with José Mourinho very few times. The last two times he'd done so had been for the match against Sparta Prague for the Champions League the year before, and for the game against Polonia Warszawa for the UEFA Cup during the current season. Porto had lost on both occasions, and Silvino had been given the nickname 'cold foot', which he found difficult to shake off.

I'm so convinced we're going to win tomorrow, that 'cold foot' will be on the bench

The day before the match, the FC Porto coach announced, *"Silvino will be next to me on the bench."* Immediately, some 'fearful souls' started whistling skyward, suspicious and afraid of what the gods of misfortune might mete out, now that FC Porto's goalkeeper coach was to sit on the bench.

José Mourinho smiled and stood his ground. *"I'm so convinced we're going to win tomorrow, that 'cold foot' will be on the bench."* Silvino himself was afraid, especially since he knew that some people weren't happy about it, but Mourinho would not change his mind.

"We won 6-1, and every time we scored a goal, 'cold foot' would tap me on the arm and smile sarcastically as if to say, 'Right, now I want to see who'll have the guts to keep on calling me 'cold foot'."

And that's when this nickname was finally dropped.

There couldn't have been a more perfect match to follow their first defeat in the League, and FC Porto had practically made it to the quarter-finals of the UEFA Cup.

Their next match, three days later at Antas would prove to be decisive for José Mourinho's team. This was the first Portuguese League match after their first defeat, and after that they would be facing Benfica at Luz Stadium. In addition, Jorge Costa and Costinha were banned for this match – a ban relating to the previous Benfica-FC Porto match played at Antas, where there had been some 'misunderstandings' with Simão Sabrosa. Deco couldn't play either, as he'd been sent off in the match against Marítimo. Furthermore, Mourinho couldn't count on Nuno Valente either as he was injured. It was therefore important – vital even – to arrive at Luz Stadium with a 10-point difference. And so they did. FC Porto beat Beira-Mar 3-0, and arrived for the game at Luz 10 points ahead of their closest rival.

Guaranteed their place in the next qualifying round of the UEFA Cup, the match against Denislizpor in Turkey, which ended 2-2, was nothing more than an opportunity to rotate some of the less used players. It even made it possible for the Hungarian, Akos Busakis, from the B team to make his debut.

Despite this match in the middle of the week, all attention was really focused on the game to be played at Luz. Mourinho knew that a loss wouldn't jeopardise their position, but that a draw or a win would hand the championship to FC Porto.

He was so sure of this, that a week before the match José Mourinho told me, *"If I don't lose at Luz, we will start writing a book detailing my journey as head coach. I feel that if we draw, at least, the League will have been won."*

Even though he believed a draw would be enough to make them champions, his ambition soared higher still. He wanted to win at Luz. To do so he had to convey a message of ambition to his players that would leave them in absolutely no doubt: they had to win!

And so, right at the beginning of the week, some players were – or maybe not – surprised by the training practices.

"In order to boost player morale, I'm not usually the type of coach who says things like: 'let's get them, we're better than they are, we'll walk all over them, etc, etc.' For the Benfica match, however, the message I transmitted was one of complete superiority over our opponents. I wanted them to feel that they were better, and had everything in their favour to win.

At the beginning of the week I started the practice by rehearsing moves made by the opponent and how we would quash these. I also knew that every time Benfica were losing, Camacho would substitute Zahovic with Sokota. So, with this in mind I started preparing my team for Sokota's attacking moves, until a rather surprised player told me, 'But, Mister, they don't play with Sokota, they play with Zahovic!'

It was precisely what I had wanted to hear so that I could reply, 'They play with Zahovic when they're winning. Against us they'll have to play with Sokota, Camacho's option when they're losing.'"

In terms of the media, however, the match began way before the scheduled hour. José Mourinho 'hitched a ride' with Simão Sabrosa to get himself into a controversy, which proved pretty useful. The only thing Mourinho feared were dead balls, as Benfica had excellent players to deal with these. In his comments to journalists, Simão had said that Benfica were stronger than FC Porto. Mourinho immediately responded by saying, *"If they're stronger, then let that be reflected by them spending less time on the ground."* So, although it wasn't the FC Porto coach who initiated 'hostilities', Mourinho took advantage of the situation to send out a message about the only issue that really concerned him: the faking of fouls by Benfica players, which might lead to free kicks near the goal area or even penalties.

Having done their homework and with player morale on a high, José Mourinho returned to Luz Stadium for the first time since he'd left there at the end of 2000.

"As soon as I got off the coach at Luz, the first person I saw and greeted was João Salgado, president Vilarinho's advisor. And so my return began in a calm and polite manner. Then at the entrance to the changing rooms, there were many people waiting for me – masseurs, groundsmen, kit men, the breakfast lady – just loads of people waiting for me. I felt proud, as if I'd made some mark at Benfica to be welcomed this way.

However, I knew that when I went onto the pitch there'd be another clamorous reception – this time negative, of course. So I made a point of walking on alone, before the team. The stadium was already full when I walked on the pitch at Luz for the first time on 4 March 2003. There was still around an hour and a half to go before the game started.

It was fantastic. An amazing feeling. I had never been a first-class player who could feel, for example, what Figo had felt upon returning to Barcelona, and so I had no idea what it would be like to have eighty thousand people whistling and jeering at me.

I believe that when we are mentally strong, those people who seek to intimidate and disturb us have exactly the opposite effect. Instead, they give us the strength and courage to carry on our way. Upon hearing the whistles and jeers with which the Benfica supporters greeted me as I stepped onto the pitch at Luz, I felt as if I were the most important person in the world. At the same time, by 'taking it out' on me, they spared my team, which was also important."

When Mourinho returned, the Porto players were already beginning their warm-up. They all laughed and some even joked with the coach saying, *"Now it's our turn. Let's get out there, because the Mister has already had his share."*

And FC Porto, who were head and shoulders above their opponents, won 1-0. It was said that the score did them no justice as they had dominated the game, and once again everyone was overcome by the Porto team's clear superiority.

The next day I began to write this book on José Mourinho.

> A HUGE DISAPPOINTMENT

With the Portuguese Championship 'settled', with 13 points between Porto and second place, and after a morale-boosting win at the home ground of their main rivals, José Mourinho immediately focused his attention on another crucial phase of the season.

The next two matches would be the quarter finals of the UEFA Cup and the Portuguese Cup. Now the Porto players could concentrate on these two competitions without, obviously, ignoring the League where there were still matches to be won. José Mourinho began to think that it was possible to win other titles. The match against Benfica had made this possible. *"The game at Luz helped to resolve the Portuguese League decisively, and thus allowed us to start concentrating our efforts on another two objectives – the Portuguese Cup and the UEFA Cup – which up until then had been secondary objectives."*

Four days later, FC Porto faced Varzim at Antas in a match for the Portuguese Cup. They thrashed them 7-0 and were assured their place in the semi-finals, where their next adversary was Naval 1º de Maio from Figueira da Foz – the team that had eliminated Sporting at Alvalade.

Another match was scheduled for 20 March, and it would prove to be the biggest disappointment of the whole season. FC Porto were at home to the Greek team, Panathinaikos, and were considered favourites. They were expected to do well in this UEFA Cup match. Morale was high, and it didn't cross anybody's mind that things wouldn't run smoothly at home.

"We had everything in our favour to win the match. The Portuguese League had been resolved, we were in the semi-finals of the Portuguese Cup, the team's morale was extremely high as a result of the recent wins, we could once again count on Costinha who had been injured, and we were playing at Antas. I would have been happy with a 1-0 win although I felt that everyone wanted more."

FC Porto only had one thing working against them: the pressure of having to win at home, because of the results their opponents always managed to achieve when they played in Greece. The second leg would be at Panathinaikos' stadium – where the Greek team had never lost a single match in any European competition. In the recent past, they hadn't suffered any losses at home in the Champions League, and in the previous season they'd managed an honourable draw against Real Madrid. It was clear to the Porto team that a bad result at Antas would force them to make history in Greece.

However, not all games go well. At Antas, Panathinaikos' defensive play was impressive, whilst FC Porto missed an absurd number of chances. Finally, with twelve minutes to go, the Antas Stadium 'froze' as Olisadebe scored the goal, which would hand victory to the Greek team.

When the Italian referee brought the match to an end, José Mourinho walked over to the opposite bench to greet Sérgio Markarian, Panathinaikos' Uruguayan coach.

"When I got to where Markarian was standing, I found everybody celebrating as if they'd won the final match in the Champions League. The entire Greek delegation was celebrating, and when I found the coach I saw him with his hands held up to the sky repeating the words, 'Thank you, God' in Spanish.

Faced with that scenario, I reacted instinctively and told him, 'Don't get carried away; this isn't over yet.' He looked at me surprised, and thinking I had been offended he said a little clumsily, 'No, no, I know… it isn't over yet…'

What I had in mind was to put him under pressure as soon as possible, and I continued with my 'attack' there and then. 'My team plays very well away, and so this isn't over yet.'

Once again, Markarian's charm came through, and calmer he now said to me, 'No, this isn't over. Congratulations, you have a fine team.' After this short but incisive conversation, I headed towards the exit and walked past the Superdragões.[19] *At that moment, what I had hoped for was, in fact, taking place. I'd secretly hoped that when we lost at Antas for the first time, people would recognise we'd done everything to prevent this. Not only did this happen, but the team left the stadium to a clamorous ovation.*

I turned round to face the Porto supporters group, and signalled to them with my hands as if to say, 'Be calm. We still have something to say in Greece.' I was made to remember that in the days that followed, up until the match in Greece. People would see me in the streets and say, 'Mister, don't forget you said that this isn't over yet. We have to go there and win, we believe we can…'."

19. Superdragões – literally means Super Dragons. One of FC Porto's supporters groups.

And believe they did. The next match, which Porto won 2-0, was for the Super League against União de Leiria. When Mourinho walked onto the pitch an enormous banner could be seen in the Superdragões area which read: *'IF ALL OF YOU BELIEVE, THEN SO DO WE'.*

And so a pact was sealed among the Porto family: everyone believed that it was possible to get to the semi-finals. In fact, immediately after the defeat, José Mourinho was the first to ask people to believe. When he arrived in the changing rooms, after witnessing the Greek celebrations, he was faced with the complete opposite. His players were downcast and frustrated, their heads hung low. Mourinho wanted to set things straight.

"This isn't over, and I have just told their coach exactly the same thing. We're going there and we'll turn this round, and if anybody here doesn't believe that it's possible to win there and move onto the semi-finals, say so now, because you'll stay here and I'll take somebody else with me to Greece."

In the changing rooms, everyone understood José Mourinho's message perfectly. The secret lay in the fact that the players didn't feel that their coach was just talking for talking's sake. They all realised that José Mourinho believed wholeheartedly in what he was saying.

They started preparing for the second leg even before their match against Leiria. This is where one of Mourinho's advantages lay. As the League had already been settled, the Portuguese coach was able to spare his players, unlike his Uruguayan colleague. Markarian's team were fighting for the Greek title, and at that stage Panathinaikos and Olimpiakos both had the same number of points. On a physical level – and it seemed likely that the match might run into extra time – FC Porto were at an advantage. It had also been possible to build morale among the 'troops'. All that was needed was to win in Greece.

José Mourinho opted for a change in tactics. In Porto, he had adopted the usual 4-3-3 formation. In Greece, he changed to a 4-4-2 formation.

"It was important for us to have more players than them in the midfield. Normally, my reasoning would be, 'As I need to attack, I have to play with an extra forward.' But, for that match I saw things differently. 'I have to win, but I must have an extra man in the midfield to control the game.' The players accepted this situation very well. Deco himself, who was going through a rough patch in physical terms, could have more freedom to attack

without wearing himself out as much in terms of defending."

And FC Porto once again played at their highest level in Greece. They caught their opponents by surprise and scored 16 minutes into the first half. In terms of qualifying for the semi-finals, they were now tied. Immediately after Porto's goal, Vítor Baía made what was probably his best save of the season. The defensive triangle composed of Jorge Costa, Ricardo Carvalho and Costinha was superb. The midfielders were in complete control of the entire match, and the forwards silenced the impressive Greek atmosphere.

When Derlei made it 1-0 for FC Porto, the ever-confident Portuguese coach simply thought, *"That's it! The tie is ours, we're going to make it."*

Deep down, Mourinho felt that even if the others scored, his team needed to score only one more goal. From that moment on, he could play with another objective. To score, but knowing that if they conceded a goal, this wouldn't change things significantly. They were tied, and one more goal would put them ahead.

When the 90 minutes were over, FC Porto were still winning 1-0, which meant the game would go into extra time. During the brief rest period, Mourinho's speech on the field was short and direct.

I simply thought "That's it! The qualifier is ours, we're going to make it"

"Don't be afraid of a penalty shoot-out. I don't want you to feel pressurised to be all over them in order to avoid penalties. I want you to play without taking risks, waiting for the right moment. Up at the front we have Derlei and Marco Ferreira, two very fast players who didn't play against União de Leiria. An opportunity is sure to arise in 30 minutes. We'll wait for it, and settle the game there and then."

The opportunity arose 13 minutes into the first half of extra time. Again Derlei didn't squander it. In the second half, both sides were visibly tired, but were FC Porto to concede a goal they would still have made it to the semi-finals. And so, they focused on maintaining their advantage.

> THE BEST MATCH OF THE SEASON

The draw for the semi-finals was to take place the next morning. The other qualifiers were Boavista, Glasgow Celtic and Lazio. José Mourinho was in no doubt as to which opponent he preferred.

"If the objective was only to make it to the final, then I wanted anyone except Lazio. If the objective was to win the Cup, then I wanted the Italians. So I felt that the draw would favour us either way. If we got Lazio, the UEFA Cup would be an objective to attain. If we got Boavista or Celtic we'd aim to get to the final, and then we'd see what would happen once there. So, I was calm about the draw."

And they got Lazio in the draw, almost as if Mourinho was being pushed towards the final victory.

However, before the match with Lazio, which was still 23 days away, FC Porto had the Portuguese Super League to win. Ahead lay an away match in Madeira against Nacional, and another against Vitória de Setúbal at home. They kept to the same philosophy for the Portuguese championship, that is *"the sooner we were champions, the better, but we would go into these matches with no pressure, and we would manage the squad and the 13-point lead we had on Benfica."*

In Madeira they won 2-1, and at Antas there was yet another win, this time 3-0. Now FC Porto were only three wins away from winning the Super League.

Four days later, they were facing a much more complicated encounter: the Lazio of Cláudio Lopez, Sinisa Mihajlovic and Fernando Couto, coached by a former 'giant' of Italian football, Roberto Mancini.

One thing that worried José Mourinho about this match was that Lazio would score. Knowing Italian football as he did, the Porto coach knew that often a goal away meant winning the qualifier. The Italians are, perhaps, the strongest in the world when it comes to defending, and once they've scored their approach shifts to merely defending. To penetrate an Italian defence and score is always very complicated. So, Mourinho felt that a goalless draw at Antas wasn't necessarily a bad result. However, he didn't want to have the pressure of needing to win in Italy in order to win the knockout round. He also knew something that nobody else did. Every time a team of his had come up against Cláudio Lopez, the striker had always scored. This had happened eight

times in Spain, when Mourinho was Barcelona's assistant coach and Lopez had played for Valencia. One of those matches had been the semi-final for the Champions League. José Mourinho would never forget the hat trick pulled off by Cláudio Lopez, which meant Barcelona didn't make it to the final. Unsurprisingly Mourinho feared Cláudio Lopez, not because he was at all superstitious, but because Lopez really was – and is – an excellent striker, and one of the fastest he'd ever seen.

And once again, 'Piojo' Lopez didn't 'disappoint' Mourinho. Fourteen minutes into the match, in a counter-attacking move, he was already in Porto's penalty area when he got the ball. He immediately took a shot that was impossible for Vítor Baía to stop. It was the worst possible way to kick off the qualifier against Lazio. Usually, a team that starts this way doesn't win.

"At that moment, I thought that if we could still win 2-1, it would be a spectacular result. In the worst-case scenario, I wanted a draw. But a 4-1 win never once crossed my mind.

Hope began to grow when I saw my team's reaction to that goal. They remained unperturbed and kept the same pace of play as if nothing had happened. They scored soon after, bringing the score to 1-1. However, this result still meant I'd have to go to Italy to win. I wished then, more than ever before, that my team would score again, which they did before halftime."

The second half proved this match to be the best of the season. Their shaky start didn't rattle the team, who went on to annihilate Lazio. The final score was 4-1 in favour of the Portuguese.

Towards the end of the match, already into injury time, José Mourinho found himself sent off – and justifiably so.

"There were only one or two minutes left to the end, when in a counter-attacking move the ball went over the sideline, very near to me. The Argentine, Castroman, immediately picked it up and got ready to throw it to a team-mate of his. He was in line with the edge of our penalty area and I realised the danger this posed. Our defence was at a disadvantage; that is, there were two Italian forwards to my two defenders, who would soon be joined by Castroman who'd also take part in this attack. A 4-1 win was an excellent result, but 4-2 wouldn't be that good. He was very near me, and I pulled him so that he couldn't throw the ball in immediately. The Argentine reacted, the referee saw this and he did what he had to do: he sent me off and gave the Lazio player a yellow card.

Obviously, it was ugly. My reaction hadn't been instinctive, and so I admit the referee was right to have sent me off. This wasn't a show of 'fair play' on my part, in addition to my having intervened directly in the match. I apologised to Castroman on the spot, and he smiled and simply said, 'Mister, it's football.'"

On his way to the changing rooms, Mourinho was walking behind Vítor Baía's goal when the referee blew his whistle for the end of the game. Under normal circumstances, the 4-1 win would have been enough to ensure a place in the final. However, FC Porto's coach hadn't forgotten that they still had a match to play in Rome fifteen days later.

In the meantime, there were still the semi-finals of the Portuguese Cup to be played. While União de Leiria were at home to Paços de Ferreira, FC Porto would play the sensational Naval 1º de Maio at Antas. Many still remembered the game against Sporting at Alvalade, including the Porto players and coaches. Forewarned is forearmed, and Porto didn't give their opponents any chances, thereby guaranteeing their place in the season's first final with a 2-0 win.

Three victories away from winning the Super League, the match against Moreirense meant Porto were now only two wins away from this target, as the scoreboard registered a final result of 2-1. They maintained the same philosophy of squad rotation, as Lazio were soon to follow.

For the game in Rome, UEFA banned José Mourinho as a result of his expulsion in the previous match at Antas. And so he was not able to speak to his players from the moment they stepped into the Olympic Stadium right to the end of the game. These are the norms of the European Football Federation.

A banned coach cannot go to the changing rooms before or during a match. To make things worse, UEFA placed a 'guard' in the stands two steps below Mourinho, to guarantee that the coach would not communicate with his bench during the match. A problem that had to be overcome.

"I tried to foresee everything that might happen. Tactical changes during the match, risky situations for them such as to be 2-0 ahead in the final moments and needing to score another goal to win the qualifier, players being sent off, and even doctors going on and what advice they could give. Basically, we tried to foresee everything. I have never prepared for a match as well as for this one. It was an attempt to cut down the unforeseeable to a bare minimum. I watched countless Lazio games, even those against much weaker teams, in order to study them in situations where they were clearly superior and didn't fear their opponents. I knew Lazio inside out.

I tried to foresee everything that might happen. I knew Lazio inside out

The only thing I didn't foresee was our own bad luck. Two days before the game, I lost Costinha when he injured himself during a practice. Under those circumstances, he was an essential player because he spoke to me a great deal, and he liked to understand the practices, the whys and wherefores. Thus, I had thought that in my absence, Costinha would be a vital player, as he would convey my ideas on the pitch. Costinha would basically be my 'assistant coach' on the pitch. I lost this possibility, but I would like to emphasise the important role played by Vítor Baía and Jorge Costa, for the leadership they displayed on the pitch and for the stability they were able to transmit to their team-mates. I believe they were truly decisive players."

But there were more surprises in store. The FC Porto coach was still to go through a rough patch.

"The big shock came when we arrived at the stadium on the coach and I said goodbye to them. They headed for the changing rooms, and I stayed behind watching them. I had to make my way to the stands. What it came down to was that I wasn't going 'into battle' with them. It made me cry, and it's a feeling I never want to experience again. I cried because I couldn't be 'in the war' with my men."

And later, it was almost unbearable for Mourinho when in the stands the Porto supporters wanted to show him all their support, and the esteem they had for him. When they saw him, they tried to speak to him, to ask for his autograph and to take his photograph. Mourinho, however, was already concentrating fully on his work and hadn't yet got over the shock of being separated from his team. The result was that he didn't act in the way that he normally did, and there was no reciprocation of the affection and support that the Porto supporters had always shown him. It was the most agonising moment in José Mourinho's entire victorious journey to the UEFA Cup.

It was then that he thought about one of his players, who could not take part in the game either. Costinha was lying in a hospital bed in Oporto, and taking advantage of this moment of solitude and anguish, José Mourinho sent him a text message saying, *"Costa, I feel bad, very frustrated. They're down there getting ready and I'm far away from all of them. Very sad."*

Costinha immediately sent him a text back. *"Be calm, Mister. They know what they have to do. Be calm."* From then on, even during the match, Costinha continued to send encouraging text messages, and the coach felt a little more cheery.

There was still a match to run, even from a distance. Prevented from communicating in any way with his team by UEFA laws, Mourinho had to get round this.

Today, the marvels of technology make it possible to speak in real time using your fingers. A little different from the method Mourinho had sarcastically proclaimed publicly when asked how he would speak to the bench and the players. The 'smoke signals' had been replaced by something much more efficient and much less polluting.

He sat in the stands between Lima Pereira and André Vilas Boas – each of whom had a small, sophisticated telecommunications device. As the UEFA spy kept an ever watchful eye on him, José Mourinho had no choice but to speak to his assistants in a normal and relaxed manner: *"Be careful, close in on the right"* or *"Look out, there's no one marking Inzaghi"*, and so on. Mourinho's words were immediately written down and sent to the substitutes' bench, where they were received by another sophisticated device. And so, José Mourinho was able to lead his team on-line from the stands in Rome's Olympic

Although forbidden by UEFA, new technology allowed Mourinho to send these messages to the bench

- Tell the players where I am; I want them to look at me before the game.
- Deco on Liverani, can't let him play.
- Maniche cannot pressurise so far away, Maniche doesn't go after Liverani. When Paulo opens, Aleni must be close to Maniche.
- Helder's sleeping, must keep up with César.
- Midfield must be full whether we've got the ball or not, Maniche late in supporting.
- If one of the midfielders is on the sideline, Maniche covers his area.
- Hold onto the ball, Deco must play more, shout.
- Score in the crossings, Aleni, must also follow Stankovic.
- Protect Nuno Valente more, he's not well, Aleni and midfielder close by when they come in with ball.
- Deco must stop inventing moves.
- Tell Deco I'm pissed off, I want more!!!
- Warm up Marco Ferreira.
- Marco depends on Derlei; if he's well Marco sits.
- Tell them five minutes left.
- Tell them time again, total concentration.
- Pressure on linesman, everybody.
- Watch Lopez, know where he is, look out for depth and also when he moves to receive us it's to turn and kick, also look out for corners.
- Derlei in wall instead of Hélder Postiga.
- For Oddo to surge forward, Gianni becoming third defender, Aleni must be on Oddo, as Gianni stays in position. V. important.
- Deco more fixed, no longer 2nd striker, must close for Aleni to sway.
- Warm up Tiago and Marco.
- Ricardo careful, Lazetic fast.
- Switch the warm-up guys with the others; don't let them get carried away, total concentration.
- Change substitutes.
- Dino Baggio lots of attention to dead balls.
- Tiago in Aleni's place, Aleni in Deco's place, Deco off. Teach Tiago to rotate in the wall with Vitor.
- Change the warm-up guys.
- Jankauskas for Derlei with same functions for dead balls, including wall.
- Jankauskas wait, only in 40th minute.
- On with Jankauskas, Derlei off.
- Pedro Emanuel free, behind the two midfielders, Aleni off, Maniche, Paulo Ferreira and Tiago remain in midfield.

Stadium, and it was from there that he saw his players come to a goalless draw, putting the club from Antas in a UEFA Cup final for the first time. Jorge Nuno Pinto da Costa became the first club president to ensure his presence at the four European finals (the UEFA Cup, the Cup Winners Cup, the European Champions Cup and the European Super Cup) and the Intercontinental Cup. José Mourinho also began to make history as the first Portuguese coach to qualify for the UEFA Cup final. Now, they had to win the Cup. The match over, Mourinho believed that this was a goal within the reach of his players.

"Five minutes before the end of the game I felt we'd make it through to the final. I left the stands and went to the changing rooms to await my players. The Lazio players were the first to walk past me in the corridor, and in a great display of fair play they greeted me and acknowledged FC Porto's superiority. Then my players started arriving, and contrary to what people may think, there were no big celebrations. They were happy, but they weren't euphoric or ready to party. At that moment, the ambition of a football team was there for all to see. The final was no longer enough for them. Nothing had as yet been won, and so there was little to celebrate."

By that time, José Mourinho knew that Glasgow Celtic had beaten Boavista 1-0 at Bessa Stadium and that the Scots were to be his opponents in the final.

"I was sad for Boavista and its players, but from a football point of view I preferred Celtic. At the outset, it would be more prestigious for the final win to be over Celtic. Beating a Portuguese team wasn't the same as beating a Scottish team – especially a Portuguese team that was languishing in mid-table, many points away from FC Porto.

I was sad for Boavista and its players, but from a sports point of view I preferred Celtic

Also, in terms of the quality of play, I thought Celtic would be better. A match against Boavista in Seville would never be a great final. In fact, I recall our game at Antas against Boavista, which was, I feel, the ugliest match I'd seen that season. I thought Boavista would consider us as the stronger team, and would play a defensive game, marking players and not taking great risks in terms of attack. We knew each other very well, and so there wouldn't be much room for surprises. All of this made me think that it would be easier to beat Celtic than Boavista, while at the same time ensuring a great game."

Back home, FC Porto were only four points away from being champions. Two days after their European match, their next League match was against Académica. They'd done their homework, but didn't play as well as they could have. They drew, and so the next match against Santa Clara would be the one that could give them the title. A win the following Sunday would result in them being confirmed as the home champions.

They prepared intensively during that week; the game against Santa Clara was a 'final' to be won.

> THE FIRST TITLE

The second half of the match against Santa Clara had barely started. 48 minutes into the match. Hélder Postiga shot, and goalkeeper Jorge Silva wasn't able to hold onto the ball. Derlei, the 'Ninja', didn't allow the Santa Clara keeper a second chance; he moved swiftly and brought the score to 3-0.

Banned from the bench, José Mourinho was sitting high up in the presidential box of the Antas Stadium. He felt, even though there were still 42 minutes left, that nothing could strip him of the 2002/2003 National Championship title. He looked across at his wife, said nothing, and threw her that serious look that she knew so well after the many years they had shared together. He looked, curled his lips, and held her hand tightly. They had sealed yet another commitment: the commitment of champions. He felt the title was not his alone. He sat with his wife, Tami, and their two children, Tita and Zuca, who sat between them watching the match. This victory was also theirs, as they had always stood by him, even when he was away. At that moment, both parents exchanged a glance, and felt that the four of them were champions.

José Mourinho relaxed, and uttered his first words. Very few, as usual. *"Tami, we've made it."* Then he grabbed his children and kissed them, as he finally laughed, all the while hugging them and repeating, *"Dad is a champion, we are all champions. We won't lose the title now."*

The noise was deafening in a stadium full of ecstatic supporters. FC Porto were once again titleholders, three years after their last victory.

In the 77th minute, Deco, the 'Magician', scored again. There was another "explosion" of happiness in the Antas Stadium. Mourinho chose this moment to get up. It was time to join his 'tribe' in the changing rooms. Moving slowly and surely, he tapped his wife on the shoulder, bent down and kissed her. *"I'm off. I'm going to give the president a hug and I'm leaving,"* he whispered. He kissed his children once more. Below him, many VIPs had come into the presidential box and were congratulating Jorge Nuno Pinto da Costa, the president of Porto's victory. Both men, coach and president, looked at each other – few words were necessary. They knew each other well, and they knew what this moment meant to both themselves and the club. They hugged each other, and said almost secretly:

"Congratulations, Mr President."

"Congratulations, Mister."

The party continued in the box, while on the pitch the match went on. As he stood at the door of the presidential box, he turned round for one last look at his wife and children. None of them saw the last smile of a husband and father, a reserved but happy smile. Happy about everything and for everyone.

He had fulfilled the prophecy he'd made a little over a year before, when he had been presented as FC Porto's coach: *"I'm sure we will be champions next year."* At the time, he had no idea that this sentence would be brought up by his opponents until the day he became champion. On 4 May 2003, Mourinho closed this chapter.

He took the lift down two floors and left the Antas Stadium. It took him a few minutes to make his way to the entrance of FC Porto's changing rooms. When he walked in people were already celebrating. He felt a need to 'be a part' of that group – those anonymous people who aren't on the bench, but who are still crucially important to a team's success. Group 'culture' is an essential aspect of José Mourinho's method of working. Those who were celebrating 'backstage' – kit men, masseurs, groundsmen and others – were just as important as him. So, for a few intense moments, José Mourinho joined these humble and unknown people in their celebration, people who were also champions.

'We made it!' was heard rising above the shouts and hugs

The game continued as he headed for the players' tunnel that leads onto the pitch at Antas. On the way, he phoned his parents in Setúbal, who were quick to congratulate him. With a partial view of the match that was still going on, he saw someone whom he considered to have played a special role in the 'blue and white' victory – Nelson Puga, one of the

club's doctors, known as a 'dragon through and through'. José Mourinho and the doctor exchanged a long and heartfelt hug of recognition and gratitude.

In the meantime, the match was coming to an end, and more and more people were gathering at the end of the players' tunnel, around the FC Porto coach. Silvino Louro and Rui Faria, Mourinho's assistant coaches, were there, as were Antero Henrique, from the club's Image and Communications Department, and many others.

"We made it!" was heard rising above the shouts and hugs.

Surrounded by the happy confusion that reigned, Mourinho still managed to capture another magical moment. With a clear 'image' in the midst of this out-of-focus atmosphere, José Mourinho heard the whistle blow twice as the referee, Elmano Santos, brought the match to an end. Immediately, there was another explosion – perhaps the greatest – which came from the stands. Instinctively, José Mourinho raised his arms in a sign of victory, and was literally engulfed by a crowd who wanted to congratulate him, there and then in the players' tunnel. Much was said in that tunnel, during those moments, but a simple sentence will forever be etched in José Mourinho's memory: *"We made it, Mister!"*

The Santa Clara players and the officials were the first to leave the pitch. FC Porto's directors had prepared a celebration, and were eagerly waiting for the new national champions to come off the pitch. Still in the tunnel, Mourinho too awaited his players. A few minutes later they began to arrive: Baía, Jorge Costa, Postiga, Deco and all the others. They came into the tunnel as they had gone into the game: fast and furious, taking everything along with them. More hugs for Mourinho, this time from his players.

There followed a rush of emotions, hugs all round, songs and even tears. José Mourinho, however, took some time to stand back and observe. He wanted to celebrate, but he also wanted to watch the celebration and savour the moment as a spectator.

A few metres away from him, Marco Ferreira and Paulo Ferreira hugged each other and shared a few tears. They had recently followed the same path. Both had played for Vitória de Setúbal in previous seasons. The former had arrived at Antas mid-season, while the latter had been there from the start of the season. José Mourinho approached them both, and in an all-embracing hug he joined in the moment. The first to speak was Paulo Ferreira, a man of few words, of whom Mourinho has often said that he *"doesn't know what his voice sounds like."* Somewhat emotionally, with a mixture of happiness and pride, he said, *"Mister, have you seen how far we've come? And to think that we started off as the underdogs."* Then it was Marco Ferreira's turn to speak. He said three simple words:

"Thank you, Mister."

At that moment, José Mourinho felt that it had all been worth it.

The celebration at Antas looked set to last. While the squad headed for the changing rooms to put on the T-shirts commemorating the championship win, a stage was being set up on the pitch. It was there, in the changing rooms, that José Mourinho congratulated his players one by one. Jorge Nuno Pinto da Costa also arrived at that moment, and took part in the celebrations, although he is usually a president more in bad times than in good. That may be why he didn't stay long.

Finally, they made their way back onto the pitch. José Mourinho felt more than ever what it is to belong to FC Porto. He looked around and heard the deliriously happy crowd shouting his name. He heard and saw everything in silence, as if removed from it all. This was undoubtedly a chapter in his life to remember. He tried to take in the colours, the movements, the music and the shouts. He tried to hold onto the images and the sounds of the vibrant, even frenetic, crowd forever – a crowd that was shouting out his name. Then he looked up, and there on high, were his wife, Tami; Tita, who shares her mother's name, Matilde; and Zuca, who has the same name as his father, José Mário. Mourinho could see them clearly, and knowing they were looking at him, he held up his hand for a long time, giving them the 'thumbs-up' sign. Tami knew all too well what he was thinking.

"It was perhaps the most magical moment of the evening. The children and I were up there in the presidential box, and he was down there with the players. That was when everybody in the stadium disappeared, and we were there alone. Without speaking, we understood each other perfectly. I knew what he was thinking at that precise moment, and he knew what I was thinking. Zé Mário has never been one to show his feelings much, so I have learnt to 'decipher' him, sometimes from a single gesture, expression or glance. So, even without saying much or being close to me, I was able to understand him that night, and know what he was going through and how he felt about this occasion."

Pinto da Costa also took part in the celebrations, though he is usually a president more in the bad times than in good

Meanwhile, the party continued below. On the improvised stage, placed in the middle of the pitch, the players, coaches and directors were now celebrating. José Mourinho was showered with champagne several times and carried off by his players. In the stands, excitement took over the crowd as the fans stayed put. José Mourinho realised that many of the fans were increasingly shouting out his name. He felt 'drawn' to the spectators, and for the first time he felt like a star. He ran a slow lap around the stadium, near the perimeter fence and close to the fans. As he went round, the crowd in the stands got up and did a Mexican wave in slow motion, as they cried out in unison the name *'Mourinho'*.

"There aren't many words to describe what I felt. You feel small when you hear your name being shouted by around forty three thousand people at the same time. The feeling is indescribable. Then, I was suddenly exhausted. I had

run slowly for about 400 metres, whereas I run much more than that during practice and don't get tired. At that moment, when I got to the end, I was exhausted – as if I'd run a marathon. That single lap around the Antas Stadium was filled with a lot of emotion and tension."

But José Mourinho didn't stop there; he had to do one more lap without having recovered from the first. The coach looked around and saw the rest of the coaching staff, the medical team, the kit men and the other people involved in the daily work at FC Porto. Hand in hand, they all set off on their lap of honour, their road to glory. Once again the blue-and-white crowd cheered them on, all the while singing, *"Champions, champions, we are the champions."*

I might go on to win many more titles, but this one is special... it's the first

Back in his office, Mourinho was alone. He turned on the television and waited for Tami and his children to arrive. He sat down, relaxed and for a moment thought about the next game, which would be against Paços de Ferreira. He immediately promised himself that this was a day to celebrate, and so he would not allow himself to think about work now. This was a celebration, and he would continue to celebrate. He would leave his office and make his way to the restaurant in Oporto, where he and the rest of the squad and their wives were to party way into the night.

Domingos Pereira, an FC Porto employee, brought in Mourinho's wife and children. He'd gone to fetch them from the presidential box and now here they were in the coach's office. In a calmer and surely more familial atmosphere the family was once again together, but not for long. The children went home and José and Tami headed for the party.

Alone in the car, the closeness between them could be felt. With José Mourinho football is always on his mind. The woman to whom he is married knows that's the way it is and always will be.

"Even at home, he is always talking or thinking about football. The game is always on his mind. We used to go out for dinner after the matches at Antas. When dinner begins, he asks me about my day and the children. Then, halfway through he is already talking about football, and by dessert he starts drawing up the team and the strategy for the next game. That's what he's like,

and there's no way round it. He'll always be like this."

The celebrations in Oporto were already in full swing. Blue-and-white flags and scarves had begun to invade the city. As he made his way to the private party being held by the FC Porto trainers and players, he realised that the car behind him was honking relentlessly in the occupants' desire to party and celebrate louder and more than anyone else. José Mourinho looked in the rear-view mirror, and let himself be carried away by the contagious happiness of those who were celebrating behind him. And, for him, that is one of the greatest prizes – to know that somewhere there are happy people out there, and that he in some way contributed to it.

Tami interrupted his train of thought.

"Look at all the excitement in this town."

"Yes, and this time I'm largely responsible for it. I might go on to win many more titles, but this one is special... it's the first."

"And it certainly wasn't easy."

"It's never easy to win the national championship. Whether we're talking about the players, or the coaches, we've all got a history that has brought us to this point. If I hadn't been on a certain path, I might never have got here. You know Tami, more and more I am sure that winning the national championship never starts on the first day of the league. There's a history, made up by each of us, that leads us to that final victory. It's that history, in its entirety, that turns us into champions. Without knowing it, all of us

celebrating together tonight, had already begun to be champions some years back – perhaps before we even dreamt of one day working for FC Porto."

After the title-winning match, all concentration focused on the UEFA final, but there were still two matches for the Super League. One was in Paços de Ferreira, where the team faced their second loss, and the other against Varzim. In both of these matches José Mourinho didn't use any of the players that would play in the UEFA Cup final in Seville – with the exception of Vítor Baía.

FC Porto started training specifically for the European final immediately after the match against Santa Clara.

"I tried to 'save' the players for the final, but not only. Essentially, the players didn't compete for two weeks because of the type of preparation we underwent for the final. If they had played in the matches that came between the game that sealed our victory in the Portuguese League and the final in Seville, they wouldn't have been able to train specifically the way they did. I'm speaking mainly about fitness training, where it would not have been possible for them to train so intensely if they'd had to compete, as well."

Given the preparation, motivation and the quality of work carried out, José Mourinho was increasingly convinced that they could and should win the final.

His confidence and certainty were so great, that a week before the final he was quite clear when he said, *"We're better, our morale is high and we're well prepared. We've got everything it takes to win and we will win. No other result will satisfy me. I just wish this were the last match of the season. From Seville, we'd go straight on holiday, and celebrate as much as we liked."*

> THE FINAL IN SEVILLE

(This section is written by José Mourinho)

19 May 2003. Two days before the grand final, we left Antas and headed for the airport. It had been a fantastic week of work, with specific training aimed at the final. There'd been individual training for each player in terms of his position; tactical work had been pushed to its limits, taking the unexpected into account; and a psychological analysis of each man had been carried out. My team were strong, very strong – impervious to disbelief and doubt; firm in their tactical approach to the game; physiologically adapted to Seville's climate

as a result of a week's training between 12:00 and 1:30 pm; and immune to all the euphoria surrounding them. As we say in Porto, *"We were like steel."*

All doubts about Costinha and Nuno Valente had been dispelled and the 4-4-2 formation option had long since been confirmed and systematised. Under great secrecy, we had applied it in our training practices against the B team, which played using the same system and game plan as our Seville adversary. In order to make up for Hélder Postiga's absence, many thought of Jankauskas, but for me it was quite clear that wasn't the path to follow. Edgaras hadn't played for a few weeks, and given his build and playing characteristics, he'd be perfect to take on the Scots. In my opinion, to put Jankauskas on, would be to give them exactly what they wanted; that is, we'd reduce the unexpected and I'd lose the possibility of having a striker on the bench that I could use in the match in case my ideas and game plan did not work out. I wasn't certain, though, about whether to play with Capucho or Marco Ferreira, and I got onto the coach that took us to Oporto airport with this doubt still on my mind.

The messages 'Go for it Zé', 'Good luck Dad' and 'You're going to win Dad' gave me even more strength

We were to fly to Seville in the same Air Luxor Airbus 340 that had taken us to mythical Athens and brought us back from Rome. Our coach had already left for the Andalusian capital two days before with all the necessary materials and equipment. My two assistants, André Vilas Boas and Lima Pereira, were also on the coach with computers, multimedia projectors, screens and – most importantly – all the video and PowerPoint clips we would watch in order to study every defensive and attacking move of our 'enemy' down to the very last detail. The word 'enemy' – even in inverted commas – may seem rather strong, but the possibility of playing in the final and making Portuguese football history was nothing short of a battle.

When we arrived at the airport, there was a huge crowd waiting for us. We didn't say a word to the journalists. It was very clear to me that the 'message' would have to be conveyed closer to the match, and so the press conference scheduled for Seville would be the perfect time. As always, Tami and the kids were with guardian angel, Domingos Pereira.

We arrived in Seville after a short and peaceful flight, and went through the same ritual I knew so well from my days with Barcelona. The same intense heat, the same journey, the same amount of time waiting for our bags. You could sense the final was around the corner. There were posters, foreign television crews and shouts of encouragement from the fans who'd travelled with us, as well as shouts from Celtic fans who were waiting for us.

A kiss and a tight hug, sealed with messages such as *"Go for it, Zé"*, *"Good luck, Dad"* and *"You're going to win, Dad"* gave me even more strength and courage for the difficult struggle that lay ahead. I will never forget the words of encouragement from Tami, Tita and Zé.

I left the airport quickly, looking cold and distant, and giving rather curt answers. The final started there and then; I was already focusing on football alone. The UEFA Cup was the only thing on my mind.

When we arrived at the hotel, everything was perfect. Antero Henrique and Luís César don't fool around and always do a good job. The rooms were fantastic, with a motivating décor. Also, around a hundred Scottish fans were staying in the same hotel as us, which was great. I wanted my players to get a feel for the match as soon as possible, and as security would make it impossible for our opponent's fans to get too close to us, this was exactly the sort of atmosphere I was looking for. It was good for my players to feel the 'atmosphere' of our opponents. In order to emphasise the 'obsession' with this match, we arrived and got down to work. We viewed the first video – a compilation of other European matches Celtic had played. This was the first lesson: a comparison between the experimentation on the field during training and the images before them. The players understood what I was saying as never before, and watched the images, too. At that moment, I felt that they wanted to play, that they were ready to 'eat them alive'.

In the usual and inevitable outing to relax and unwind (which I wouldn't give up on, not even in Seville), we were able to watch some Scottish channels doing live broadcasts, and were even asked to do brief interviews. But we were not at all forthcoming. Still walking in the streets, we were feeling incredibly motivated. The Cup had to go back with us to Oporto. My 'platoon', solid and confident as ever, continued walking, 'protected' by three watchful security guards who were there to help us.

In the distance, the contours of the Olympic Stadium, the stage of our dream, began to take shape. There was a thrill of emotion, mixed with Silvino's

'clowning around', André Vilas Boas' innocence, Rui Faria's sarcasm, Dr Puga's fanaticism, Aloísio's silence, and the laughter of the others.

The day before the match, we got up early and had breakfast first thing in the morning, followed by another meeting. We needed to select our opponent's tactical attacking combinations and decide how to handle these effectively. We also had to choose defensive adaptations and go over how to make the most of them. This required even greater levels of concentration, and the players responded very well. We were headed in the right direction and the players assimilated everything perfectly. There were no doubts, only certainties. Afterwards, we went on a cultural outing. The theory that isolation increases concentration was firmly rooted in FC Porto, as in most clubs. This meant no outings, no contact with the outside world. Another golden rule was hotels far away from the city. I did away with all of that. With me, we stay in hotels in the city centre and we go on outings – where everything is perfectly organised in terms of time, control and access. The grand Plaza de España was the spot chosen for our stay in Seville. Some of the factors I tried to instil within the group were: relaxation, no stress, contact with the outside world, getting a feel for the Scottish fans and their reactions and, last but not least, access to culture. The days when players only got to know their hotel, the stadium and the airport are a thing of the past.

After lunch they rested, then had tea and only trained later that afternoon. As for me, I'd already been to the only press conference scheduled before the match in Seville. I left the hotel after lunch and headed for the stadium, together with Antero Henrique. It was an impressive reception, and the grandness of the occasion was to be seen in the coverage given by international television stations and by the number of journalists present. I felt strong, determined and prepared, and was aware of the message I wanted to convey: *"Confidence and determination, allied to psychological strength with regard to the pressure placed on us by those who considered us to be the favourites."* Our season was won and it had been fantastic, irrespective of whether or not we won. My players deserved all my pride.

There's no doubt. These guys are at their best, no one is afraid, they all want to play

At night, my words were devoured on the Internet, that companion during the solitude imposed by training.

In the meantime, the practice at the end of the afternoon went as I'd expected: the players concentrated well, kept up a good pace, and were physically and mentally alert. They also communicated, showed some aggressiveness, and were oblivious to the hundreds of journalists, who followed the training session so closely that it seemed they wanted to train with us. 'Old' André turned to me and said, *"There's no doubt about it. These guys are at their best, no one is afraid, they all want to play."* Capucho was in fine form. He was confident about the match, as well as calm and motivated. Marco Ferreira was exuberant, quick and determined. Halfway through the session I made the only decision that still needed to be taken: Capucho would play from the very start instead of Marco Ferreira. Capucho is more similar to Hélder Postiga in the way he moves. When Marco goes on, it will be to 'tear into' the match by the time exhaustion has begun to sink in and the heat in Seville has sapped all the energy from the muscles of the Scotsmen. At that moment, I even thought that this 'Marco' might go down in history, that's how decisive he'd be.

We returned to the hotel and were happy to see the Portuguese fans arriving. There were more and more of them in the city. Once inside the hotel, a security guard told me, *"Mister, go outside. You have a visitor in a taxi." "Who?"* I asked as I walked towards the door. There they were – my kids – tanned by the sun in Seville during their adventures in a children's park, and as always looked after by 'super mom'. I kissed them and before saying goodbye for the last time until after the match, it was my turn to reassure them. *"Don't worry, we're going to win."*

After dinner, we finally held our most important meeting. I announced the team, and presented the game plan on PowerPoint, situation by situation, what to do, how to react, how to adapt, how to win…

The night air was warm when we went out later, and the 'footballing' atmosphere was taking over the city. Already, I was thinking and dreaming about the game, visualising it, without seeing or hearing the fans who followed us – all the while under the watchful eye of Fernando, my protector and friend, and much more than a security guard hired to support us. He's one of us!

Later, in the hotel rooms, a much deserved rest for the warriors. I got a lot of faxes from friends, institutions, clubs and even from a few colleagues. It's important and fair to thank people. More than a personal assistant, Rui Silva is a companion. Delighted with his baby girl, who was only a few months old, he was always there for his annoying, demanding and emotional *Mister*. My warm thanks to him, too.

While the players rested, my coaching staff and I had our last meeting of the day. We defined everything for the next day, and I still had some time for reflection. Yes, there was time to think about where I was, how I'd got there, what I'd been through, and about the history we were about to make. I had told the players, *"Finals were made to be won"*, and I had vowed to myself that I couldn't let it slip away. I slept peacefully that night.

The great day arrived and I awoke happy, calm and confident, with my heart beating steadily, and aware that I could convey the necessary tranquillity to my players. The first meeting was a 'compact' of the dead ball situations where many of our fears lay. They posed enormous risks, and so there was still much to be taken care of. In dead ball situations, Celtic are dangerous and automatic. Baldé, Sutton and Mjallby: we defined who to mark and foresaw how they'd behave. The only situation beyond our control was Costinha's injury – Costinha who was supposed to mark Larsson during corner kicks. Thereafter we went to a park alongside the hotel, which was closed off so we could be alone. Rui Faria started the stretching session, which I would always take part in. We spoke and laughed, but we worked. More than ever before, I felt that the group was united and happy. The message that we should enjoy this final had got through. The players were alert and open to feelings and emotions. The time was fast approaching. All that was left was lunch, a siesta, tea, and a short meeting.

When we came to that magic moment – the last, short meeting before the match – I didn't make a long speech.

"Only by keeping our emotions under control, can we win finals. We have to be true to ourselves, always. We've come this far as a team and we must play as a team.

We will have the capacity to excel, and three hours from now it will all be over, we'll get the Cup and go home."

"GOOD LUCK" shouted Jorge Costa, as he always did every time I finished speaking. My captain, the man who since childhood had always gone to Antas with a FC Porto flag and scarf, had dreamt about this moment. Later, after the final, I gave him a photo of him lifting the UEFA Cup skyward, on which I wrote: *"As from this moment on, you are a legend in this club"*. We left the meeting and made our way to the coach. The game had already 'begun'. The streets were full of people and the stadium was filling up. As usual, I was the first to arrive onto the pitch of Seville's Olympic Stadium. I looked for my loved ones, who were in the stands, and I found them. I did so with the help of the camera and zoom lens belonging to Paulo Santos, a photographer for *A Bola*. The three of them were sitting together with the players' wives and children, in the sun in the side stand. I'm afraid this is the only criticism I have in relation to FC Porto's organisation. Our loved ones deserved better. I don't think that the wives and children of the Celtic delegation were in any side or upper stand, without catering, with the sun in their face and with no help at a social level. As for me, I was offered seats in a box but I didn't

As always, I kissed the photo of Zé and Tita, as I heard the whistle blow for the start

accept them out of solidarity with my players. Always with them!

I wandered around the pitch, concentrating and pensive, but with the knowledge that my family was present and united. Tami and the kids on one side, and my parents, nieces, nephews, father-in-law, relatives and friends on the other – all united by one feeling and desire: to see me win. I knew that.

During the warm-up, I sat in the chair of the TVE [20] reporter who was on the track. My president was sitting next to me, and said, *"We have to win!"* This feeling was not new to me. *"We're going to win,"* I replied, knowing that was what he wanted to hear. I returned to the changing rooms, and standing at the door were Andy Roxburgh, UEFA's technical director, and Joseph Venglos. They were waiting to greet me. Andy had been my instructor in a UEFA course and I said, *"A Scotsman wishing me luck?"* He answered in a low voice, *"I'm doing it in my capacity as a member of UEFA."*

The players returned from the warm-up. Shouts of encouragement echoed through the changing rooms, and the sound of boots hitting the floor was heard, whilst the more vain among them glanced in the mirror and the more faithful said one last prayer. Our hearts were invaded by a unified shout: *"Who are we? Porto! Who are we? Porto! Who are we? Porto!!!!"*

I was already sitting on the bench. Zé Mário had brought me some water and wished me luck. It's his ritual. I looked at Tami and the kids, opposite me, but on the other side of the stadium. As always, I kissed the photo of Zé and Tita, and at the same time I heard the whistle blow for the start. A bomb could have gone off, I wouldn't have known. I was only thinking about, smelling, feeling and living for the game.

The game began as I had expected: everything was tight, undefined and

20. TVE – A Spanish television channel.

aggressive. In the opening minutes, there was a challenge by Costinha, a violent tackle by our adversary and a muscular injury to the thigh caused by a violent collision. *"I'm done for!"* I thought. I didn't have another midfielder to compete in the air with the long ball and direct play of the Scots. So, we had to resort to another solution: Ricardo Costa on the outside and Paulo Ferreira in the midfield, changing places with the shorter Maniche. Dynamic and great in character, Maniche couldn't, however, compete in the air with Chris Sutton. If we wanted to take charge of the match and hold onto the ball, here was yet another reason to do so, as without Costinha our defence had been weakened.

So, we played with total defensive control, consistent pressing, and as much ball movement as possible given the aggressiveness and physical strength of our opponents. In this way, we created some opportunities and played with confidence – lots of confidence and determination – and adapted perfectly to the atmosphere, which was heavy both climatically and psychologically speaking.

1-0! Derlei scored at the end of the first half. It was a goal that perfectly reflected the characteristics of the players involved. Deco's telegraphic pass, Dimitri's first-class shot at the goal, and the 'Ninja's' follow-up shot. It all seemed so perfect. A minute later, the referee blew the whistle for the end of the first half. I left quickly because I wanted to structure my talk to the players. The players arrived in the changing rooms in an uproar, as a result of the Luso-British taunts directed by the Franco-African Baldé, who wanted to 'tear into' the 'Ninja', the Brazilian, Derlei. But Baldé came up against a little 'monster', born in the crib next to Dom Afonso Henriques [21] – Nuno, a great goalkeeper and a great man, who managed to get things under control when it was necessary – leaving no one in any doubt.

With all the players in the changing rooms, my ideas were clear. *"If time passes and they begin to take risks, let's wear them out physically with our ball possession, and let's kill the match with the second goal or by sending on either Marco Ferreira or Clayton."*

Jankauskas had injured himself in the last minute of the training session, and was therefore not an option. Thus, in order to attack we had the speed of the two 'cyclists'; then there was Tiago to strengthen the midfield, César Peixoto to set up and possibly decide the dead ball situation, and the great Pedro Emanuel, whom I could count on for any given situation.

The game resumed and Celtic scored. Had the Porto team lost its concentration? Had Larsson committed a foul? I don't know, but we were faced with the harsh reality of being level once again. It was back to square one. The issue now was to see how they would react to the 'green hurricane' sweeping over the stands. Here was the chance to see 'my' Porto, strong and determined, confident, arrogant and wounded.

I thought, that's it and now we're going to score

We were on top of them once more, and again we had Deco, the 'Magician', Capucho's ability to hold the midfielder, a move by Alenitchev, and a subtle touch towards the goal. I thought, *"That's it, and now we're going to score."*

I couldn't believe it when two minutes later Celtic scored again, and from a dead ball situation. What sheer frustration. My players were so well prepared and still they were being punished. Playing without Costinha was no excuse. Another player had been chosen to cover and he had failed. He apologised from afar, he knew he was the one. I gave him a 'thumbs up' to let him know that everything was okay; what we had to do was to carry on fighting. When he was closer to me, I told him, *"Don't let yourself be influenced by that mistake."* I thought about changing things and making a substitution, but they didn't let me. Soon after, Jorge Costa felt he was rather limited due to muscle fatigue and a serious contusion. Thus, having Pedro go on was an obvious option, which guaranteed me stability. Nevertheless, making this second substitution worried me as we were faced with the possibility of the game going into extra time. I needed the players to outdo themselves; I needed Nuno Valente to endure the pain. I believed they could.

21. Dom Afonso Henriques – Portugal's first King, known as 'The Conqueror'.

In the last minute we resorted to offensive pressing, we regained the ball quickly and I thought, *"Alenitchev is going to finish this off"*. In a position to score, he took a shot and kicked both the ball and the ground, and we went into extra time.

There were lots of liquids and quick stretching exercises all round.

"Come here, gather round. I want to talk. Drink lots of water and relax, but listen to what I have to say."

So, I told them, *"These are 15-minute periods. If we score, there are a few minutes left before we can take the Cup, and we have to kill ourselves out there on the field and defend. If we concede a goal, play directly to Capucho. Capucho, you have to lose the first ball on purpose so that the midfielders can get the second one and we massacre them from that position.*

But above all I believed in Vitor, we'd win on penalties

If there are no goals, play as a block, because with all this exhaustion we cannot stretch the team or stop playing along close lines. I'm going to send Marco on in a few minutes. Make him run.

Marco, I want lots of diagonal passes from the outside in. Don't mess me about by playing with the ball on your foot. If you're going to play with the ball on your foot, then I'll leave Capucho where he is."

The first minutes saw a balanced performance from both teams, and in this way we made it to half-time. Derlei came up to me and said, *"I'm finished. If you want me to press and play in the collective way we agreed upon, I can't do it. If I try, I'm either going to fall or hurt myself. I can only keep going, if I'm up at the front. If you want me to graze, I'll stay, otherwise I can't take it anymore."*

"Okay, 'Ninja' graze all you like up at the front; maybe something will happen."

That's when I started thinking about penalties. Costinha and Jorge Costa had already gone off, César Peixoto hadn't gone on yet and neither had Clayton; this made it difficult for me to choose. But, above all, I believed in the great Vítor Baía, the one I had met upon my arrival at Antas in '93, and who was back to playing at his best. We'd win on penalties! The first to score would be Ricardo Costa, then Maniche, Nuno Valente, Marco Ferreira and Derlei.

UEFA CUP
revigres

I looked at the pitch and saw Maniche with the ball. Penetration among the midfielders, a deep diagonal pass by Marco Ferreira, the goalkeeper comes out and a rebound to Derlei. Was it a goal? I don't know; I didn't see the ball go in. The bench foresaw it and jumped up in front of me. Such emotion and jumping about. Today I still can't describe it. I knelt and wept for fifteen or twenty seconds, I'm not sure – enough time to realise that I had to get back to the match. I made my way back to the bench, and returned to firmness and reality. There were instructions to be given: *"Don't defend from behind, they're tall and will massacre us. Defend on the outside, as far out as possible, rest with the ball, touch the ball, and, above all, a lot of emotional control. The game isn't over."*

In injury time, Celtic made a dangerous move, Nuno Valente chose to commit a foul and was sent off. I quickly said, *"Marco Ferreira is full of energy, he must take up the left back position."* The free kick was taken, the ball flew over the goal area, the referee blew his whistle and there was utter madness.

I started looking for my loved ones. They were ecstatic, I couldn't see them but I knew they were there. I cried because I wasn't able to hold and hug them. Later I found out that the suffering had been unbearable: my father had spent most of the time outside the stadium with his grandson, Zuca; my wife Matilde had been the bridge that united the family; and Tita had been one of the few who'd coped with the stress and watched the entire match.

We were the champions, and I was the first coach to take the UEFA Cup to Portugal. I'd gone from being a Portuguese coach to being a world coach.

The Cup was already in our hands, and we couldn't hold back anymore – we had to let it all out. I looked up and saw a vast cloud of blue, moving up and down like never before. Holding my medal in my hands, I ran towards them: members, supporters and fans, who had always supported me. I ran around excitedly and heard the crowd shouting my name. I felt they were closer to me than ever before. Still with the medal in my hands, I couldn't stop running and I jumped so much and so many times that I thought I was touching the sky. And I was. Then I stopped in front of my family. Once again, I couldn't see them, but I knew that they were there. Down on one knee, I kissed the medal again and held it up high. That was my family moment, where in my mind the whole stadium had gone silent and I could only hear them. *"We're going to win, Dad." "We won, my daughter!"*

Later, at the airport was the magical moment when I met up with my family

once more. It's a moment that is etched in my memory forever, and which was captured in a magnificent photo by David Augusto from the newspaper, *O Jogo*.

Back in Oporto, it was sheer madness: the airport was invaded, the streets were teeming with people and the stadium was full to capacity. It reflected the emotion of those who'd stayed and was a tribute to those who'd shouted our names and that of FC Porto until they were hoarse – so loudly that you could almost hear them in Seville.

Unforgettable! But let no one say unrepeatable!

> THE PORTUGUESE CUP

In the Portuguese calendar, Porto and Leiria had fifteen days to train between the last match of the Super League and the Portuguese Cup final.

After having played Sporting, Mourinho decided to hold their training period down on the Algarve. The climate was more similar to that in Lisbon, and above all he wanted to remove the players from the atmosphere of great euphoria that was sweeping the country's football capital, Oporto.

Once down on the Algarve, life was calm and centred around work.

Mornings were spent in the pool, and the afternoons practising. After dinner, the players were free until 11:00 pm. One day, José Mourinho gave his players the evening off, and found that the season was ending just as it had begun. The FC Porto players decided to go out for dinner together and once again they made it back to the hotel several minutes before their 11 o'clock 'curfew'.

However, not everything ran smoothly. During their first practice, something happened that could have shaken the team: Derlei seriously injured himself in a collision with Jankauskas, and fractured the zygomatic arch in his cheekbone.

Everything I'd missed out on, everything I'd stopped doing and all the hardships now made sense

"We immediately thought that Derlei wouldn't be able to play in the final. However, I must once again highlight the swift action taken by our Medical Department, which was vital and decisive for the player's recovery. At around 6:00 pm Derlei was lying on the pitch and Dr Puga called Oporto in order to arrange the operation for that very night. Then, they still went past Faro Hospital, so that they'd already leave with the necessary X-rays. Derlei went off to Oporto with painkillers and an ice pack on his face. They got there at one in the morning, at two he was in the operating theatre, and by three they were calling me to say that everything had gone well and not to rule him out of the Portuguese Cup Final just yet. When the doctor told me that, and what with Derlei being the person that he is, I immediately thought, 'He's going to play!'"

During the second week, training was held at Antas behind closed doors, so that no one would know that Derlei was to play after all.

In the last training session before the final, Mourinho asked Silvino to work with Derlei on his finishing. After taking some shots at Vítor Baía's goal, the assistant trainer said to Derlei, *"Now a few cross shots with the head."* A wary Derlei asked, *"With the head?"* Silvino replied, *"Just one or two slow balls and then we'll go."*

Half an hour later, they were still at it, with Derlei more committed than ever before as his headers made their way into the goal area. It was exactly what José Mourinho needed to see.

After having trained the whole week, the 'Ninja' played in the final for the Portuguese Cup. The only restriction on Derlei was that he couldn't take part in dead ball situations, where there is always a great deal of physical contact and an elbow in his face could have been disastrous. For the second corner, as the 'Ninja' could no longer take it, he swopped with Maniche. From thereon in, he didn't lose another dead ball situation.

Porto won 1-0, and among the 'treble' festivities, there was Derlei, the 'Ninja' and 'matador', celebrating the win and the goal he had scored against União de Leiria. He'd been a decisive player once again.

Porto, both club and city, celebrated yet another title. At some point during the night, José Mourinho stopped to think, if only for a second – another chapter in a story of successes had closed.

"I felt tired but happy, proud and rewarded. I came to the conclusion that I'd taken the right steps along the way, that I'd made good choices and that the investment had been worth it. Everything I'd missed out on, everything I'd stopped doing and all the hardships now made sense. The reward had finally arrived."

» CHAPTER VI **ON TOP OF EUROPE**

FC PORTO 2003/04

IDEAS FOR A NEW SEASON
THE SEASON KICKS OFF OFFICIALLY
A DEFEAT THAT LEFT NO MARK
DERLEI'S INJURY
THE MATCH OF ALL LIES
THE ICING ON THE CAKE
AN INSPIRED NIGHT
A PREMATURE CELEBRATION
THE PORTUGUESE CUP FINAL
THE CHAMPIONS LEAGUE FINAL
THE MOVE TO CHELSEA

>> CHAPTER VI **ON TOP OF EUROPE**

At the end of the 2002/03 season, FC Porto were enjoying one of the best moments in their history. Euphoria had swept over everyone in the city of Oporto. Fans, directors, coaches and players were still wondering how it had been possible to fulfil their dream of winning the Portuguese League, the Portuguese Cup and, above all, the UEFA Cup. The media spotlight was now focused on those players who, just a year before, were *"poor and badly paid, but young and full of ambition and hungry for titles"*. In twelve months, the situation had changed quite dramatically. The Porto squad was now older, better paid and boasted many more titles. All that was left now was to test their level of ambition. For José Mourinho there was no other alternative. His 'tribe' had to remain ambitious, and any player content with a UEFA Cup win would definitely not fit into his group. Thus, their previous victories could only be viewed as a stimulus to renew their conquering spirit. The 2002/03 season had been *"unforgettable... but not unrepeatable"*, and so there was room to do better still – but only if ambition was high. What then was going on in his players' minds?

He thought about this for the first time a few days after having won the European trophy, before anyone had yet gone on holiday. The Mayor of Gaia, Luís Filipe Menezes, wanted to pay homage to the champions from Antas, and had organised a dinner for the entire FC Porto delegation at the city hall. During the ceremony, José Mourinho officially confirmed he'd be staying on with Porto for another two years. At the end, players and coaches stepped onto the FC Porto bus; the players on the top floor, and the coaching staff and the rest of the delegation below. In the still of the night, during the trip that would take them to Antas, José Mourinho looked out of the window and contemplated the city of Oporto across the bridge. There stood the mother-city of all the victories they'd won and those that were still to come. The season that was drawing to a close was not the end of the dream, but rather the beginning. He could sense the happiness coming from the top floor, and knew he had to find out how far his players were willing to go after these days of glory. To think they'd won everything, to live in the shadow of the past, and not to go further was very little for someone who still had a lot to give… and to win. He came to an immediate conclusion: *"I won't let them be dazzled by all of this. I'm going to demand even greater ambition and humility. This is the only way we can continue to win."*

It was at that moment that José Mourinho started to prepare the next season, even though the 2002/03 one wasn't over yet. He spoke with all his staff, preparing them for the change in his players' personality. The danger was that the past could rob them of their future.

"I may be exaggerating, or maybe I'm completely wrong in what I'm about to say, but I think that prevention is better than cure.

I have no doubts whatsoever that I'm ready for conflict, but nobody is going to have an easy ride with me just because they won some titles. You have to help me, so that together we'll know how to deal with this new situation in our lives and how to fight against any temptation to be dazzled. We must always keep our emotions under control, both individually and at a group level, otherwise we'll be halfway down the path that leads to defeat."

The staff listened carefully. Only time would tell how the team would react to the success they'd achieved. The bus came to a stop, and FC Porto went on holiday.

> IDEAS FOR THE NEW SEASON

On 14 July 2003, Porto's season started. During the holidays, José Mourinho couldn't stop thinking of the danger of their being dazzled, so much so that he *"was very well prepared to deal with"* that possibility.

The season didn't get off to an easy start. There were even some 'signs' that worried the coach.

"I remember there were some players who'd never arrived late for any meeting or practice before and now they did; some wouldn't practise because of a little muscular pain, whereas in the past they'd always trained; others wouldn't take any criticism about 'fair play' they'd previously displayed. These were signs – not great problems – that those who worked with me and I were ready for and reacted to immediately.

In order for things to get back to what they'd been, I took two decisions during the pre-season. I sent Serginho away because he returned almost eight kilos overweight, and 20 minutes into the match against Hanover I substituted Maniche because I felt he hadn't reacted in the best way to some criticism I'd made from the bench. I intentionally took these decisions to provoke reactions."

This perhaps helps to clarify a statement made by Mourinho, which was widely reported: *"I need to know if success has harmed us in any way."* The risk that this problem might develop was greater, in that the team for the new season was basically the same as that of the previous season. There was a clear investment in continuity, and there were no 'new faces', something which often boosts internal competitiveness and, ultimately, renews ambition.

I needed to know if success had harmed us in any way

FC Porto kept their champion team practically intact, and only Hélder Postiga left, as he was transferred to the English League. However, José Mourinho wasn't overly concerned about this departure for various reasons. The strongest – perhaps – was the strong possibility of Porto being able to sign Benny McCarthy. Between Postiga and the South African, Mourinho clearly preferred the latter since *"unlike Postiga, McCarthy is a born finisher"*. It was thought the game plan would benefit the flanks, with players like Derlei, César Peixoto and Maciel (at the time everyone was convinced he'd still arrive during the pre-season) getting the ball into the centre of the goal area, where McCarthy would be a key player in this tactical scheme. However, these plans came to nothing as a result of injuries sustained by both Derlei and Peixoto, which would keep them off the pitch for several months. Furthermore, Maciel would only arrive in December. On the other hand, the Club would make a considerable amount of money, as the sale of Postiga would more than cover the fee for signing McCarthy.

Another two players would also leave the squad: Capucho, of his own accord, as he hadn't played much in the 2002/03 season; and Clayton, who was exchanged for Sporting's Ricardo Fernandes. The former Sporting player was chosen as Mourinho felt he needed more options in midfield. Following this logic, yet another two players were signed: José Bosingwa from Boavista, and

Pedro Mendes from Vitória de Guimarães. José Bosingwa, at a press conference on 2 August, was the first to foresee great things for the new season. When asked about the future and how far the 'new' FC Porto could go, he replied with a question, *"Why not win the Champions League?"* Imagine if José Mourinho had said this.

Unlike his player, the coach never made winning the Champions League an objective for the new season.

"I'd be lying if I said that I thought about winning it. Having won the UEFA Cup did, in fact, give us a certain status, but it wasn't enough to allow me to make winning the Champions League an objective. In this regard, I thought we absolutely had to make it through to the second round for three reasons. Firstly, to consolidate the prestige we'd achieved the previous season; secondly, for the financial rewards it would bring the Club; and thirdly, each of us would have a greater impact at a European level than we already had. As far as I was concerned, making it to the second round was an obligation. Once we got there, my objective was to eliminate a great European team at any point. That would be 'the icing on the cake', and I'd feel that I had fulfilled my duty in relation to the Champions League."

José Mourinho is a coach who develops constantly. His ideas, training methodology and concept of play are systematically analysed and studied, and are continuously evolving. He has progressed in such a way that he clearly states that he is not the same coach today as he was at practices two years ago. The end of every season is a landmark, and he invariably spends the holidays studying and preparing for the future. No matter how good the previous season, there are always changes to be made for the next one – nothing stays the same.

There were two game plans from the 2002/03 season: the 4-3-3 formation used for the Portuguese Super League, and the 4-4-2 formation FC Porto had played in the UEFA Cup. This difference in tactics had come about as a result of the increasing difficulties they'd felt during the European competition – with opponents such as Panathinaikos, Lazio and Glasgow Celtic – which had made them adopt a more cautious defensive system. Thus, they had opted to strengthen the midfield. It was this strategy, which had worked so well in the UEFA Cup, that justified Mourinho's decision to kick off the new season with a 4-4-2 formation. They were certain to come up against powerful opponents in

the Champions League and they needed to have a strong back line. However, the 4-3-3 formation was still a valid option for Portuguese competitions, and so it would be necessary to refine both systems. From the very beginning, the training methodology adopted made the Porto players assimilate both approaches. This had been done the year before, but at a later stage, at the point when the level of difficulty had increased.

José Mourinho felt the team was more or less fixed: Vítor Baía; Paulo Ferreira, Jorge Costa, Ricardo Carvalho (or Pedro Emanuel as an option) and Nuno Valente; Costinha, Deco, Maniche and (maybe) Alenitchev; Derlei and McCarthy. It didn't differ from the previous team, except for McCarthy in place of Hélder Postiga.

There was, however, a problem. Given the exposure they'd attained, everyone now knew how FC Porto played, as well as their game principles, methodologies and concepts. In addition, the players were the same, from which it could be concluded that they'd keep to the same structure. So, they needed to surprise their opponents, especially in the way they played, which was why José Mourinho had prepared to 'take the next step'. How to surprise them? That's where the evolution lay. The Porto coach wanted to prepare his team to change their game plan at the slightest sign from the bench; that is, he wanted them to change from a 4-4-2 formation to 4-3-3, and vice versa, at the drop of a hat. In this way, no one would know how the team would be playing; nor would they know how they would start or finish a match. Essentially, it was about playing differently every week – and even within the same game. So, at the beginning of the Super League, FC Porto used the 4-3-3 formation in the first two matches against Sporting de Braga and Estrela da Amadora; in the third match they played Sporting and opted for the 4-4-2 formation; in the fifth match, against União de Leiria, they reverted to 4-3-3; for the fifth match;

against Benfica, it was back to 4-4-2, and so on. The 'automatic systems' had been set up, and now it was a question of perfecting them over time – injuries permitting.

> *THE SEASON KICKS OFF OFFICIALLY*

The 2003/04 season officially started with the match against União de Leiria, on 10 August. This was the National Super Cup, roughly equivalent to the FA Community Shield in England, and the trophy made its way to Antas after a 1-0 win at the D. Afonso Henriques Stadium in Guimarães. It was an important victory; it was their first real test, and a win meant another trophy for FC Porto. Not only would the match test the new methodologies they'd adopted, but they'd also be playing against a traditionally difficult team. In the end, José Mourinho would win the only cup he was missing in Portugal. They were already in the second half when Costinha scored the only goal of the match. And so, FC Porto began the season the same way they'd ended the previous one; that is, with a 1-0 win over União de Leiria. Even so, at the end of the match, José Mourinho said that his team could do better.

The Super League kicked off a week later, on 17 August. FC Porto were at home to Sporting de Braga, and two goals by McCarthy and Derlei saw them beat their opponents. This win wasn't immediately followed by another, as in the second match of the season they drew 1-1 against Estrela da Amadora, with McCarthy scoring once again. FC Porto dropped to third place in the table.

Five days later they were to play in their second final of the season. The trip to Monaco had a double meaning for Mourinho. Firstly, they were to take on AC Milan in the European Super Cup, and secondly he was to receive the UEFA prize for Coach of the Year, together with Carlo Ancelotti, his opponent's coach.

Porto lost the final 1-0, but Mourinho was pleased with his team's performance, telling journalists *"I've got my team back."*

I feel we were very well prepared when we set off for Monaco. We clearly knew what to do and how to change things if necessary. We knew our opponent's most frequently used movements in detail and, above all, we were aware of the difficulties we'd face in terms of reversing a negative result, were this to happen. But this is what football is about, and we conceded a goal only five minutes into the match. It was precisely what we feared most, not because of the goal itself, but rather because of what it means when your opponent is an Italian team.

From that moment on, we had to score; or rather they were in their element. For this reason, the match was very different to what we had expected and despite the opportunities we had, we weren't even able to draw. Obviously, we always feel very frustrated after a loss, but we were somewhat comforted by the team's simple reasoning: if Milan is tops, then we're also tops. This conclusion became so entrenched in our minds, that throughout the season everybody wanted to play against Milan in the Champions League to prove it once and for all. We lost the match, but we gained confidence for the future."

The next day, back in Oporto, the journalists spoke to José Mourinho about the European Super Cup final once more. What 'harm' could the loss have caused to the Porto team? Mourinho appeared confident, and again he tried to convey that confidence in the changing rooms. *"Sporting will pay for this"*, he said, reminding everyone that the team from Alvalade would be their next opponents in the Portuguese Super League. And pay Sporting did. At home, FC Porto thrashed the team coached by Fernando Santos 4-1. It was the first of five matches scheduled for September. The journalists spoke of a *"crazy month"* ahead; and the *"crazy month"* had got off to a good start. After Sporting, there were games against União de Leiria, Benfica and Vitória de Guimarães. There was also a match against Partizan Belgrade, in the first round of the Champions League.

The win against Sporting meant Porto moved up to second place in the Super League. Sporting dropped from first to third, and for the first time Marítimo were top of the table.

In their fourth match, Porto won once again, this time 3-1, in an away match against União de Leiria. Derlei, who had already scored against Sporting, continued scoring and began to stand out as their top scorer. In the meantime, Marítimo also won their match and remained in the number one spot, but this was only to last for another week.

The Porto-Benfica match lay ahead, as did the first game for the Champions League in Belgrade. The final result was 1-1, not the worst way to start off the competition.

The second derby of the season was set for 21 September. As always, it was a special match for both Benfica and Porto, although the teams occupied very different rankings in the table. Benfica's 10th place was rather far away from Porto's 2nd place.

"At the outset, we were in a superior position for various reasons. To begin with, the season had got off to a shaky start for Benfica, who were down in the second half of the league table. Although not serious at this stage of the championship, this was, however, rather demoralising. Then, we realised that Benfica didn't feel at ease in relation to this game. The burden of not having won at Antas for many years was also not in their favour and placed us in a better position. The spectators also play an important role. Their behaviour is special – there is a great deal of emotion – and even their affection is different when FC Porto plays Benfica. I'd say it's more than all other games, against Sporting, Real Madrid, etc. This gave us strength, and I believe it weakened our opponents somewhat. And finally, this was the last Porto-Benfica to be played at Antas, and none of us wanted to be associated with a loss in that match. We got ready for that game feeling that we had to

win in any way possible. That Porto-Benfica match was to crush them, to push them, to play well or badly, to score in the first or last minute, to score one or three goals, but essentially it was a game to be won. It had to be, and that was that!"

It was in this frame of mind that Mourinho set about preparing for the last match against Benfica at the Antas Stadium. It was a game to win – there was an added responsibility. The previous year, FC Porto had won the last match between them at Luz Stadium; they had also managed this feat against Sporting at Alvalade, as well as another win over the Lions [22] at Antas in the season under way, and now they wanted to do it again against Benfica. In this way, they would be associated with four wins in as many farewells.

I put Deco as shadow striker thus confusing our opponents

With Benny McCarthy banned, the two teams would face each other on 21 September 2003.

"Perhaps because of the loaded psychological element involved, I think we went into this match feeling a little apprehensive, and so we didn't get off to a good start. This might have given Benfica some mental strength, and they played daringly, in the good sense of the word. They were confident and started the game by playing very well. We ended up scoring a goal in each half and went on to win, but they played an excellent match, something they hadn't done at Antas for a long time."

After their fifth match, FC Porto swapped places with Marítimo to take first place in the Super League table – a position they'd hold until the very end. As a result of the loss, Benfica dropped to thirteenth place, while Sporting fell from third to sixth in the standings. The Porto team won on all fronts.

The last match of that 'crazy' September witnessed yet another victory, as Porto won 2-1 away in Guimarães. Derlei, who had scored against Benfica, did so again and confirmed himself not only as the leading scorer, but also as the best player in the competition. In the first Super League matches, he only failed to score in Amadora.

22. The nickname for Sporting Clube de Portugal.

> A DEFEAT THAT LEFT NO MARK

FC Porto suffered their second loss of the season on 1 October 2003. They were at home to Real Madrid for a Champions League match, and fate smiled down on the Spanish team, who won 3-1. It was a rather bitter game for José Mourinho.

"I think we started the match off well. I put Deco as shadow striker – thus confusing our opponents – and we were the first to score. But then their individual quality and our defensive errors proved to be deadly. They turned the score around, but I won't forget that when they were 2-1 ahead, the referee disallowed a goal of ours due to a non-existent offside. And then they made it 3-1, which finished off the game. I tried everything; we even ended the match playing with three forwards – Derlei, Jankauskas and McCarthy – but it wasn't enough. When a team is losing against Real by two goals, they know it is almost always impossible to turn things round and this affects the players' morale. At a psychological level there were no repercussions in the team, as they knew they had done everything and that, like it or not, Real are a special team, one that is very difficult to beat."

The defeat by Real didn't leave a 'mark', but it forced FC Porto not to lose the next match in Marseilles, which was to take place three weeks later. But before that there were two Super League matches: one against Académica de Coimbra at Antas; and the other against Belenenses in Restelo. Two matches resulted in two wins, and the team began to feel no one could stop them on their way to a second consecutive title. Derlei scored once more in both matches and was definitely the man of the moment, leaving the 'star' Deco out of the limelight.

The match against Belenenses called for their first, unscheduled tactical change, which not only surprised the team led by Manuel José with a 4-1 win, but was also a trial run for their next challenge in Marseilles. José Mourinho decided to leave two forwards, McCarthy and Jankauskas, on the bench, and opted for two extremely fast and creative wingers, César Peixoto and Marco Ferreira. Their mission was to pass the ball to Derlei, who'd act as a mobile striker, with Deco behind him – Deco who seemed to be returning to form.

"Basically, I wanted to make the most out of the best-ever Derlei and to

find the Deco we had previously seen. The match was so perfect that I thought I should keep to the same team for the game in France. Also, I was looking for an element of surprise, as many thought that any changes to the front line were aimed at letting Benny and Edgaras rest."

Knowing that defeat would mean going out of the Champions League, the blue-and-white delegation set off for Marseilles. A draw would be a good result, but a win would be ideal. And win they did, 3-2, in a match that was marked by the first significant injury of the season. César Peixoto tore the anterior cruciate ligament in his left leg – which would certainly keep him off the pitch for a recovery period of at least three months. The victory had a bitter taste.

"César had started to play regularly and we thought we'd found the player we wanted for the left flank. He had played very well in the previous matches; he was strong and confident; with a fantastic left foot, he crossed well and shot even better; and he was strong in one-on-one situations. Basically, he had everything we were looking for. When he injured himself, I immediately thought that in terms of the team, we'd have to return to the 4-4-2 formation, as without César we couldn't play with three forwards."

César Peixoto's injury ended up giving José Mourinho a once-in-a-lifetime opportunity. Three days later, the coach watched the player being operated on.

"I plucked up courage and was present at the operation. I felt that, given the opportunity, it was important to me and to César to be there. On my part, in order to understand what the operation entailed so that I could participate more actively in his recovery. On César's part, I think it was important for a player to know that his coach was at his side during a very difficult time in his life. Essentially, by being there I was telling him, 'get better because we're waiting for you'.

During the operation, the medical team was fantastic. As things progressed, they explained to me everything they were doing. It was a clean, bloodless operation, and so I could observe everything that was happening and perfectly understand each step they were taking. What got to me the most was the sound of the drill as it bore into the bone and the smell of burnt meat when the medical team removed the rotulian tendon with an electric scalpel. This surgical procedure made me understand the extent of this type of injury, and at the same time it conditioned some of my future attitudes. I realised that the pressure coaches always place on both the players and medical departments to speed up recovery doesn't make sense in most cases. From that moment on, I began to be more sympathetic to my players' complaints and the concerns of the doctors."

From that moment on, I began to be more sympathetic to my players' complaints

José Mourinho had witnessed his first surgical procedure. Unfortunately, it wouldn't be the last of the season.

Back with the 4-4-2 formation, Mourinho's team won their next two matches, 1-0 in each. At Bessa against Boavista, and at Antas against Marseilles in the Champions League. The latter match meant that the team moved back to second place in their group. Now it was entirely in their hands to make it through to the second round. A win in their next match against Partizan would guarantee them qualification for the next round, and even the opportunity to challenge Real Madrid for first place in the group, in the last game which was to take place in Madrid.

Back in the Portuguese Super League, Porto drew for the second time. Mourinho wasn't pleased with the game against Moreirense in Braga, which ended 1-1.

In mid November, Pinto da Costa finally inaugurated the Stadium of the Dragon. From the very beginning, José Mourinho had kept up with the work on this stadium, and had made only one request: for his seat to be higher than anyone else's. His wish was granted, and for the match against Barcelona he sat in a chair a full metre and a half above everyone else on the bench. As for the game, Barcelona weren't able to overcome the attacking power of the owners of this new stadium, and FC Porto won 2-0.

"Although it was only a friendly match, we felt that we had to win it. The Club had done its share of the work; the Stadium of the Dragon had been built. Our mission was to continue that work by winning matches in the new stadium. And the best way to start was by winning the very first match. However, the symbolism of that moment was not lost on me. Thus, taking advantage of the absence of some of the players on the National Team, I called up some 'kids' from the junior ranks to make up the team that faced Barcelona. I decided on a junior player (Vieira), a juvenile player (Hélder), and some players from the B team (Evaldo and Pedro Vieira, among others) in order to have players from FC Porto's various teams present at that moment. It turned out to be a wonderful night, and everything went off very well."

The pitch, however, was not in the best of conditions and the team would have to return to their former stadium, Antas, for subsequent matches.

"As we'd held several practices there, I was certain that the pitch in the new stadium wouldn't be up to scratch. However, the company responsible for the turf used had sent the Club a document guaranteeing that everything would be fine, and so I had to wait and see. During the game with Barcelona, it was clear to me that in sporting terms, it wouldn't do my team any good to continue playing at the Dragon. Once again, the FC Porto president showed his worth. When I confronted him with the choice between a possible financial loss or possible sporting losses, he clearly opted for the former, and so we immediately returned to Antas."

Back at the 'old' Antas Stadium, FC Porto began to defend the third title they'd conquered the previous season: the Portuguese Cup. They hosted and beat Boavista, with another goal by Derlei. The score was exactly the same as it had been in previous matches. José Mourinho had taken on Boavista five times, and on those five occasions he'd beaten them 1-0.

From Cup to Cup, four days later they were up against Partizan Belgrade. A draw would automatically qualify them for the second round of the Champions League, and the team wouldn't have to worry about the final match in Madrid. Benny McCarthy scored the two goals that sealed their 2-1 victory, and they qualified for the last sixteen. The last match of the first round, against Real,

could still place them first in their group, but that would mean that FC Porto would have to win 3-0, at least. José Mourinho was clear when he stated that *"coming top of the group is unrealistic"*.

And it was. A draw in Madrid two weeks later placed them second. Two days later, they found out that Manchester United would be their next opponents on the road to the European title. And there they were, down to the last sixteen. José Mourinho had everything he'd wished for: a great European team… to eliminate. Strangely enough, in the days before the draw, the Porto trainer had often told the press that he wanted either Manchester or Monaco.

"When the results of the draw came out, all those around me immediately said, 'Next time, keep your mouth shut'. But the truth is I really wanted it to be one of those two clubs. Monaco because I thought they would be the easiest of all to eliminate; and Manchester because they fitted in with my reasoning of wanting to beat a great European club. However, if we lost against them, nobody could hold it against us, as long as they didn't thrash us. At the time, I thought that given the way we were playing, it could go either way. So, all we had to do was to go to 'war'."

> DERLEI'S INJURY

It was now December 2003, and after a 4-1 win against Gil Vicente on 30 November, FC Porto drew for the third time in the season, 2-2 against Marítimo. After that, the team went on winning during the next month and a half, up until their match against Sporting at Alvalade. Before the end of the year, FC Porto still beat Beira-Mar and Alverca in Super League matches, as well as Maia in a Portuguese Cup match. Of all these matches, one was to leave its mark. On 22 December, Porto's leading scorer, and most influential player, seriously injured himself in Alverca. As had happened to César Peixoto, Derlei also tore the anterior cruciate ligament, but in his right leg.

"I was still on the bench when Dr Puga informed me of Derlei's condition. I remember sitting there for about a minute thinking, 'Good Lord, now what?' But I quickly got over that and once again concentrated solely on the match that had to be won.

At half-time, when I arrived in the changing rooms the atmosphere was unbearable. Everybody was quiet and shocked; they couldn't believe it. I'd even say they were in pain. But it was right there that Derlei showed his mettle. He was lying on the stretcher, and hadn't yet been rushed off to hospital because we knew he'd have to be operated on a day or two later. He called his team-mates and told them there was no reason for any drama, because a tragedy would have been losing a leg or not being able to walk again. He insisted that there was a solution to his problem and told them he'd be playing again in a few months' time. I think he even told them to 'stop all this nonsense and go out there and win the game'. And we did."

At the end of the match, José Mourinho was immediately concerned about who would replace Derlei. After César Peixoto, he now had another player who'd be off the pitch for a long time. Without at least one more player who could somehow occupy a place up at the front and manage to play along the flanks, the team's entire tactical scheme could go down the drain.

"At the time, we were already trying to sign Maciel from União de Leiria. Once again the objective was to have a 4-3-3 formation as an option for our game plan, as that possibility had disappeared with César Peixoto's injury. However, it was immediately clear to me that even if Maciel joined us, the

4-3-3 formation would never be possible without Derlei. Thus, Maciel was no longer seen – as he had been initially – as an asset who would provide us with more options; he was now an essential player to be signed, our emergency contingency. As he was different to Derlei, he could cover some gaps, especially in relation to the Portuguese competitions.

Once we'd solved the Super League problem, I started to think about the Champions League. I needed a player who could play in Portugal and abroad. Maciel couldn't as he had already played in a European match for União de Leiria. Luís Gonçalves from the Scouting Department suggested Carlos Alberto from Fluminense, and advised me to go and see him in Brazil. It only took one game for me to make up my mind about signing him."

It was immediately clear that the 4x3x3 formation would never be possible without Derlei

Within the space of a week, José Mourinho and Pinto da Costa had signed two players and resolved, as best they could, the gaps left by the absence of César Peixoto and Derlei.

The New Year saw them back in the Super League after a mini holiday. The first match without Derlei was against Rio Ave, at Antas, and apprehension swept over the FC Porto coach.

"I feel it was one of the most important matches of the season for various reasons. It was the penultimate match in the first half of the League season, and thus a turning point. Furthermore, Rio Ave had lost against our two rivals, Benfica and Sporting. Lastly, and most importantly, it was our first 'post Derlei' match, and I didn't know how the team was going to react to this. The truth is that his absence affected the team and we didn't play at all well, unlike Rio Ave who put on a very good performance. They were consistent and well organised, and didn't make any big mistakes. In the end we scored the only goal of the match in the last minute, a penalty, and I think it was the first game of the season where we were lucky.

That luck – winning in the last minute, by scoring a penalty, despite playing badly – always gives a team some confidence. So, at the end, I told my players that anyone who can win a match like that can win all the other matches that lie ahead. It was the 'little star' of champions at work."

And FC Porto won their very next games. Paços de Ferreira, Sporting de Braga and Estrela da Amadora – and in between Vilafranquense, for the Portuguese Cup – were no match for Porto's attacking and defensive power. In those four matches, the blue-and-white team scored eight times, and didn't concede a single goal.

These wins made it possible for José Mourinho to achieve his objective: to start the second half of the season with a good lead, as he would be facing two away matches against Sporting and Benfica in the third and fourth match-rounds. There was a seven-point difference separating Porto from second place Sporting, and even if they lost both matches, they'd still be in the lead – a factor Mourinho considered to be essential.

At this time, UEFA selected José Mourinho as Trainer of the Year for 2003, and it was also at around this time that he signed his last player. Sérgio Conceição was placed on the right wing, and together with McCarthy and Maciel he would offer the coach the possibility of again using three forwards in his game plan. Soon after, however, he was injured – and Mourinho's plans were again thwarted.

In the meantime, on 25 January 2004, Portuguese football was rocked by a most dramatic event. Miklos Fehér, Benfica's Hungarian forward, died on the pitch during a match. His sudden death, live on TV, shocked the country – and Mourinho was no exception.

"I was at home watching the match, and immediately realised that the situation was very serious. I phoned Dr Puga and asked him for his opinion on what was happening to Fehér. All he said was that he wasn't sure, but that it was clear to him that it was something extremely serious. I started crying, as did my wife next to me. At that moment, there was no Benfica, no Sporting, no Porto.

I went to the player's wake at Luz Stadium, with Jorge Costa, in his capacity as captain, and Reinaldo Torres, a member of the Board, and we were made to feel very welcome by the Benfica directors. I came face-to-face with José Veiga for the first time since joining FC Porto. He hugged me, which I considered normal; we had never been enemies, only distant with no type of relationship between us. At that moment, what was at stake was the loss of a human life, of a young player who was a good friend of José Veiga's.

Nothing else was important, and nothing else made any sense at that moment. Those were difficult days for everybody who was involved in Portuguese football."

> THE MATCH OF ALL LIES

Life went on, and so did football. On the last day in December, the first of two key tests finally arrived: the match against Sporting, at Alvalade.

They were already in the second half, and FC Porto were ahead 1-0. Suddenly, João Pinto fell over the sideline and collided violently against the advertising panels. It was immediately evident that the Sporting player had seriously injured himself. He was lying off the playing field and Paulo Ferreira, who was near the sideline, tried to find out how he was. The Porto captain, Jorge Costa, abandoned his position as central defender and ran towards Sporting's midfielder, who kept on calling for the medical team to come on. The players from FC Porto 'switched off' from the game. At that moment, upon the referee's indication, Rui Jorge quickly restarted play. José Mourinho's players were caught off guard, and Liedson entered the goal area. Paulo Ferreira intercepted the ball with great effort, and the linesman Lucílio Baptista awarded Sporting a dubious penalty. Sporting scored and the match ended 1-1.

A great deal was reported about this match and about the minutes described above. It proved to be the most controversial match of the whole season for José Mourinho. In the end, Mourinho was scathing in his analysis of the incident, and criticised Rui Jorge severely for having taken advantage of a moment of solidarity in order to 'betray' his opponents. According to Mourinho, the ball should never have been placed back on the pitch without Sporting allowing the Porto players to return to their positions. Sporting then 'counter attacked'. At the press conference, José Bettencourt, a Sporting director, held up Rui Jorge's shirt, which had been torn to shreds. According to Bettencourt, FC Porto's coach had torn it up in the changing rooms when the Sporting kit man sought to swap it for a Porto player's shirt. José Mourinho was also attributed with saying, *"I want Rui Jorge to die on the field."*

Is that what happened?

"After the match was over, the first bit of 'trouble' happened between Fernando Santos and me. On my way to the press conference, I ran into the Sporting coach, who was rather worked up and asked me how I could have done that and said that, etc, etc, etc. Without really understanding what he was accusing me of, I answered him the same way, using extremely harsh words. I even insulted him. I immediately regretted this, and then publicly apologised to him straight after at the press conference. But it should be said that I wouldn't do so today. In fact, after reading the declarations Fernando Santos gave to the Disciplinary Board, I now feel I could have said much harsher things to him after all.

I'm still waiting to be shown footage of everything they say I did

In any case, I immediately went to the press conference and everything took place normally, with the criticisms I then delivered.

I was already on the bus that would take us back to Oporto, when I was told that José Bettencourt was speaking to the journalists and making those accusations against me that everyone knows. Such monstrous comments stunned me. Obviously, I completely deny all of their accusations, because not once did I even see any Sporting shirts, let alone tear them; and not once did I make that statement about Rui Jorge that I was accused of.

But let's look at the facts, to understand this whole situation better.

I had access to Fernando Santos' declarations in the Disciplinary Board's report. Sporting's former coach says he neither saw nor heard anything, but that he is sure I did everything I was accused of given the agitated state I was in, as well as the way he was told what had happened. In the same report, Sporting's kit man, Paulinho, for whom I have a lot of affection, never said he

saw or heard me. He simply stated – probably under pressure – that it was the Porto kit man who told him everything. In turn, the Porto kit man, Fernando Brandão, stated he never said anything and merely swapped some shirts with the Sporting kit man. So, it's one man's word against another's. Even at the press conference, José Bettencourt didn't say he'd seen or heard anything. The fourth official, Bruno Paixão, also said he saw and heard nothing; otherwise he would have taken disciplinary action against me, which – as we know – he did not. As for me, I'm still waiting to be shown film footage or hear a sound recording – neither of which cannot exist – of everything they say I did. Up until now, nobody has shown or played me anything. So, I'm accused of having done and said something that nobody saw or heard. Thus, to bring this farce to an end once and for all, and so that no one is left in any doubt, I categorically state that I didn't tear up any shirt and I never said that I wanted Rui Jorge to die on the field!

As for the rest, I hope the courts will come to a decision. That is where the Sporting directors will have to prove all the accusations they made against me."

And that is the end of the soap opera created by Sporting at the end of a match that resulted in a draw, and about which Mourinho now confesses he had *"never seen people from a great club so happy with a draw at home for a Super League match"*.

At a football level, José Mourinho left Alvalade having achieved his objective. By not losing, he didn't allow Sporting to get any closer to Porto in terms of points.

For their next match, FC Porto returned to the new Stadium of the Dragon. The pitch was still not at its best, but they won 2-1. Mourinho commented that *"the pitch is tiresome"*, and faced with insistent questions from journalists, Pinto da Costa replied that he wasn't a gardener. It was thus decided to replace the pitch; that is, to lay a completely new carpet of turf at the stadium.

Porto were still two matches away from their final and definitive test: the game against Benfica at Luz Stadium. In the meantime, they beat União de Leiria at home and Rio Ave away; the score was 2-1 in both matches.

Talking about the match at Luz, José Mourinho reiterated what he had said around a month earlier: *"If I don't lose, I'll be a champion"*.

He went to Luz and didn't lose – in a match that was a model of fair-play.

"The game against Benfica should be an example for the Super League because there weren't any problems either on or off the pitch. We were welcomed with utmost cordiality by the Benfica Board, and even on the pitch nothing happened that could be considered less honourable. Everything took place extremely correctly, and nobody was sent off – which was beginning to be something of a rarity in the matches between the bigger teams. We scored, then Benfica drew, and there's nothing negative that can be said about that game.

At the end, there was even a foul on Jorge Costa, deserving of a penalty, which the referee did not award. However the match was so proper, that no one on my team felt they had a right to cast a shadow over it by publicly demanding that penalty. José António Camacho and I greeted each other once again, as always based on respect and a certain level of friendship that already existed between us. To sum up, it was the perfect atmosphere in a derby that is always very complicated. As had happened at Alvalade in relation to Sporting, this draw allowed me to keep the same distance between Benfica and us and assured me that first place could no longer elude me. From thereon in, it was a question of managing the lead, and thinking about Manchester United and the Champions League."

> THE ICING ON THE CAKE

That very week before the Vitória de Guimarães game, which marked the definite return of the team to the new Stadium of the Dragon, the FC Porto coach came up against a small problem in the changing rooms. Mourinho discovered the reason for Benny McCarthy's weak performance against Benfica, where the player had never got into the game and had to be substituted. Two days before the match he had gone to Vigo for his girlfriend's birthday. When this came out, McCarthy was fined and severely reprimanded by the coach. McCarthy apologised to the whole squad, and a week later he was a key player in one of the most important matches of the season, FC Porto against Manchester United.

In the meantime, the Super League game against Vitória de Guimarães proved to be an excellent precursor to the match against the English team. Porto won 3-0 and awaited the visit of Manchester United in high spirits.

"I told my players once again that I wanted any result that did not require us to win in England. To win by a goal would be good, as would a goalless draw. So we couldn't take any risks. Loss of ball possession had to be controlled; that is, it could only happen in their half of the field, and as such we'd have to move the game into that area. For me, the speed of their forwards and the way they played the offside rule to its limits, meant that losing the ball in our half could be fatal.

The other point had to do with Costinha not playing, as he'd been banned from the match. I knew that with Pedro Mendes we would lose our fighting capacity in terms of aerial play in our area of danger. Our only chance was to dominate the match, and we would have to do so up front. As for the line-up, I included Carlos Alberto for the first time from the very start as shadow striker, with total freedom to circulate along the two wings."

Mourinho's tactics, the ability of his players and a fantastic display from Benny McCarthy, who scored both his team's goals, led to a 2-1 win and kept hopes alive for the second leg at Old Trafford. Alex Ferguson didn't take kindly to the result at all, and was said to have shouted at José Mourinho, accusing the Portuguese team of play-acting and unfair play. Mourinho downplayed the accusations and understood the "psychological war" his opponent was trying to wage.

"He was aware of our team's worth and he knew that the result left him in a difficult situation. Right there, he started putting pressure on my players, as well as on the referee for the second leg match, whoever he might be. Our way of playing and the technical capacity of the FC Porto players meant the game would be physical. That's the way he wanted it, especially with the support of the home crowd. Up until the day of the match, he made that type of accusation and it was up to me to convince my players that Alex Ferguson's problem was that he was scared of us. The message I had to convey was to downplay the situation, as well as place pressure on them, saying that they had to win, not us. This was all nothing more than a psychological game between two coaches. So much so, that after we'd won at Old Trafford, Alex Ferguson, together with his captain Gary Neville, came over to the changing rooms to congratulate me."

It was also at about this time, that José Mourinho was first approached by British football. The day before the match, an agent he knew (who works closely with FC Porto), informed him of Liverpool's interest. A secret meeting had even been set up between directors and the coach, should he be available.

With the match for the last sixteen scheduled for the following day, José Mourinho declined the invitation. It wasn't yet the right time to think about the future.

Nobody risk anything; control the ball and the game, because for me 0-1 at half-time is good

"Deep down, I think I did what had to be done. I found it strange, however, that everything was being prepared and set up by someone who worked closely with FC Porto and who owed his loyalty to its President."

As for the game itself, Mourinho had clear ideas about what to expect and how he should react.

"We were prepared to play the game. We knew there would be tremendous pressure and that the Manchester United players were capable of scoring goals at home against any opponent. So, we weren't thinking about playing out a goalless draw. If that happened we'd win the tie, but we knew it would be almost impossible to come out of Old Trafford without conceding a goal. I passed on that message to the players and told them that if we let in a goal

nothing would be lost. In order to win the tie all we had to do was score another goal. When we were losing 1-0, I had to make a substitution. I put on Pedro Emanuel to replace Jorge Costa, who was injured. I was clear in my instructions to Pedro. 'Tell them on the pitch that I'm happy with this half-time result. Nobody risk anything; control the ball and the game, because, for me, 0-1 at half-time is good'. With that indication I wanted my players to believe in themselves again, as at that point in the game we were out of the competition, which could upset them and cause them to make mistakes. But there was still a long way to go and looking for an equaliser, at a difficult stage of the game, could have resulted in the second goal for the English team, and then everything would really have been lost.

Half-time came and with it, I think, a certain calm. I again reminded my players that this situation was normal and nothing had changed; that is, we already knew before the game that we had to score in order to win the tie. That was what was happening, so therefore it was nothing new. To finish off, I told them that pressure from our side would only come some 25 minutes from the final whistle, when I'd put on Jankauskas to pin down their two central defenders."

Porto's goal came in the last minute, scored by Costinha from a free kick taken by McCarthy. Porto were in the quarter finals and had eliminated a European giant. Mission accomplished?

That same week Mourinho learnt who their next opponents would be. The luck of the draw came up with Olympique Lyonnais and, should Porto make it to the semi-finals, they would meet the winner of the tie between Deportivo la

Coruña and AC Milan. Mourinho, who would have preferred Monaco, had to be content with the other French team left in the Champions League.

"I preferred Monaco because they don't have an atmosphere at home matches. It was also possible that there'd be as many Portuguese fans as Monaco fans when we went to their stadium. Olympique, however, always have a great atmosphere at home, with the crowd rooting for the team for the full 90 minutes. They were the French champions and a better team than Monaco. But we got Olympique, and right away I had to fight off the wave of euphoria that had built up around the team. The idea that it would be an easy tie came from the outside, and I did not want it to affect my players in any way. For that reason, right after the draw and upon hearing the radio and television commentary, I felt the need to head off to the Press room and say they were very strong and powerful opponents, and that the tie was far from being won."

Back to the Super League, Porto had won 1-0 against Académica de Coimbra and 4-1 against Belenenses. On the way to the title, they now prepared to take on Boavista at the Stadium of the Dragon. One goal was enough to guarantee them three points and strengthen the lead they had maintained ever since the fifth match of the season. The goal came from a sneaky free kick by Deco to the edge of the box. Suddenly McCarthy popped up, shot first time and took the Boavista defence and goalkeeper by surprise. At the end of the game, José Mourinho attributed the "ownership" of the free kick to… José António Camacho, the Benfica coach.

"I am well aware that free kick appeared for the first time in Portugal at Boavista's Centenary Tournament, in the Boavista-Benfica game. I though we could use it for our team in international competitions, as it was a well conceived free kick that surprised opponents. I didn't want to plagiarise Camacho. But in that match against Boavista the opportunity came up at a time when the game was coming to an end and we were all square. The players, who'd never had the chance to practise it in the Champions League, decided to try it out.

After the final whistle, I gave the "laurels" to Camacho. First of all, because I had an excellent relationship with him, and it was fair to 'give unto Camacho what is Camacho's'. Secondly, because a few days earlier, he had put himself in the difficult situation of stating that Porto were better than

Benfica and that if they wanted to win they had to start thinking like Porto. Thus, he had criticised Benfica and praised my team at the same time. I felt at that time the need to give him a "push" and to say that good things also came from Luz Stadium and their coach. With typical fair play, Camacho refused to accept authorship of that free kick and said he had himself seen it somewhere before."

The semi-finals of the Portuguese Cup were next and Porto beat Sporting Braga 3-1 relatively easily. At the end Mourinho declared, *"As we're the best, we'll win the Cup"*.

He did not foresee that a few months later in order to finish off the season he would have two finals to contend with in the space of one and a half weeks. Firstly, the Portuguese Cup and then the Champions League. It would have been almost impossible for one not to affect the other.

> AN INSPIRED NIGHT

It was the eve of the FC Porto-Lyon match. José Mourinho continued to advocate that in a worst-case scenario, a goalless draw would not be a bad result. In the event, an inspired night from his players handed him a 2-0 victory with goals by Deco and Ricardo Carvalho. At the end of the game, José Mourinho felt that his team were already in the semi-finals, where they'd probably play AC Milan, who had beaten Deportivo La Coruña 4-1.

"At half-time, when we were 1-0 up, I told my players that if the match was over it would have been perfect, and that if there were to be any changes, they'd need to be in terms of improving on that score. I'm from a time when drawing or winning 1-0 at home in European competitions was considered a bad result. The mentality was to win by a lot of goals at home and hold out in the away game. When you played the first tie away, then the aim was to lose by very few goals and try to turn the tie around at home. I don't think like that and I don't instil this attitude in my players. Whether at home or away, we have to play to win the game. That's all that matters.

When we won the match 2-0, I felt the tie was ours. With my team's physical, tactical and mental structure, I knew we would never let in three

goals in France without at least scoring one in return. The destiny of the tie had been sealed at the Stadium of the Dragon."

In the Super League, FC Porto could almost smell and touch the title. It was now only a question of time and the goal by Carlos Alberto against Moreirense sealed yet another victory. The next game was in Guimarães, against Luis Campos's Gil Vicente. There were seven matches left, and it looked increasingly likely that for the first time in their history, Porto would go the season unbeaten.

"Yes, that was an idea that started to grow within the team, although it wasn't an aim in itself. It would have been interesting to do it and I think if we hadn't been so involved in the Champions League we would have achieved that feat. It's just that there are some things you can't control and the fact that we were involved in three competitions was fatal. After a certain point, we started looking at the Super League in a different way. We knew we would win it, that it was only a matter of time. So we didn't "buckle down" too much. Curiously enough, we lost our unbeaten record in a game where we tried pretty hard. The team started off very well and we could have scored three or four goals right at the start. We played as we hadn't played for some time, but that's football. We didn't score and ended up conceding two goals."

As such, Porto lost their unbeaten record in the League. The team went off directly to train, because three days later they'd be facing Lyon. At dinner, José Mourinho noticed something was different. After matches, players were allowed to drink a glass of wine or beer at meals. That night, no-one asked for an alcoholic drink. On seeing this, José Mourinho stood up and told the waiter that there were no restrictions for dinner. All the FC Porto players could drink whatever they liked.

"I wanted them to understand there was no problem in losing to Gil

Vicente. I didn't think that game should result in any punishment. We lost because we had to lose at some point. It was as simple as that. So we left with our heads held high, knowing we had done everything to avoid defeat. That's the only demand I place on my players: that they give their all on the field. When that happens, you win most of the time, but you also lose once in a while. They could always have a glass when they fulfilled their duty and tried their best, irrespective of the result. To strengthen this idea, I went even further. My assistants always dropped by the players' rooms before they turned in. On this occasion, it was me. I fooled around with some of them and spoke earnestly to others. I made them realise that losing is one of three possible results in football and, even though we don't like it, we have to accept defeats stoically. And so, the first loss of the Super League was overcome as something completely natural."

The Lyon match ended up being one of the easiest games of the season. Maniche scored within a few minutes of the start and if there had been any lingering doubts, these had soon dissipated. Even with the tie effectively over, Olympique never gave up and piled on the pressure. But they had to score four goals to get to the semi-finals, an impossible task. The pressure paid off, however, and the French team got a goal in before half-time. As a precaution, José Mourinho took off Carlos Alberto and brought on Pedro Emanuel. By the start of the second half, Maniche scored again and the heads of the French team sank. They still managed to equalise, though, in injury time. The tie was won 4-2 and FC Porto went on to the semis to face Deportivo La Coruña, who had impressively beaten AC Milan 4-0 at home. José Mourinho heard of this result while the Lyon game was still on.

"Someone from UEFA told me the score. We were already in injury time. He turned to me and put up four fingers: 'Mourinho, 4-0 in Spain.' Astounded, I asked if Milan had scored the goals, to which he only replied with two words. 'No... Coruña.'

As our reserve goalkeeper, Nuno, had already played there, I turned to him and told him that Deportivo had won and would be playing us in the semis. He looked at me and said, "Mister, we're in the final!" For the first time we started feeling the responsibility of winning the Champions League. The previous day, Real Madrid and Arsenal had been eliminated and from that moment on, FC Porto were the team with the most illustrious history, the most titles won, as well as the holders of the UEFA Cup. In addition, the remaining opponents were within our reach or, to put it another way, we felt we were the strongest team left. That day our 'obligation' to win the Cup was born."

The other semi-final would be between Chelsea and Monaco.

In the Super League, a 1-0 win against Marítimo meant Porto were only four points away from becoming champions. A win and a draw – two games – would be enough. If that happened, everything would be decided before the Deportivo game. However, for the first time that season, the team drew their next two games nil-nil – against Nacional da Madeira and Beira-Mar – and the two points gained were not enough.

The party would have to wait until the second to last game of the season, against Alverca... or perhaps not.

> A PREMATURE CELEBRATION

On 21 April, the Stadium of the Dragon was packed to capacity with Portuguese and Spanish fans in what was considered by many to be the real final.

For the home tie, José Mourinho was well aware of the sort of team he was going to face: a team with a high average age, which was compensated for by a great deal of experience and a high morale as a result of the victories they'd achieved. History suggested that "Depor" managed to get excellent results in Galicia, but terrible results away from home. Their 8-3 loss against Monaco in the first stage and the 4-1 defeat in Milan were a case in point. These results led Mourinho to conclude that "*at the Dragon, they won't risk much and will stake everything on defending so as to get a result that will allow them to resolve the tie at home."*

The FC Porto coach was right in his analysis, though he couldn't foresee other factors, which ended up being decisive in the goalless draw snatched by Deportivo.

"From a psychological point of view, they started off as the better side. They were stronger which made their game more solid. On the other hand, we were inhibited at the start and didn't put into practice what we knew. We didn't develop our football. Depor's mental superiority soon became clear, and that fact affected the match and without a doubt blocked us completely. Early on I realised that finishing the game all square and leaving everything to be decided in the second leg would be a positive result. If I risked too much, we would lose."

At the end of the game, the Spanish fans in the north wing were delirious. The Galician team went over to thank them for their support. The players sang, danced, clapped and celebrated as if the tie had already been won. José Mourinho was not intimidated and now recognises, as he said at the time, that he still had something to say about the outcome – because he thought he had the better side. This was the only game that he did not manage to win at the Stadium of the Dragon.

To make up for the frustrating Champions League draw, next came the Super League celebration. FC Porto played Alverca at home while Sporting, their closest rival, played away at União de Leiria. Two points separated the Porto team from the championship. Sporting's match was about to start, when José Mourinho said that Porto could be champions without even leaving their hotel. That's exactly what happened.

"I was alone when two minutes from the end of the Sporting game a crowd rushed into the room. A party kicked off with champagne and much joy, as you can imagine. There was no rest for anyone in the hotel. I didn't forbid the partying; on the contrary, I told my players to give in to their joy, but warned them to keep an eye on the following day's match against Alverca.

On the pitch, they still had to give their all. For me, it was a question of respecting the opponent and the sporting truth, which always has to prevail. Many teams risked being relegated and Alverca were one of them. If we handed the match to José Couceiro's team, then we would have been disloyal to the other teams that had valiantly come up against us during the season. That could never happen."

We ended up winning 1-0 in a game that, to everyone's surprise, marked the return of Derlei. After an extraordinary recovery, a testimony to his willpower and character, Derlei emerged as Porto's great acquisition for the

remaining Champions League matches and the Portuguese Cup final. Both his team-mates and the fans saw in him a charismatic player, a man who always appeared at important moments and, as such, was an important psychological and sporting trump card for the decisive matches that followed.

The League had been sorted. FC Porto would lose in Vila do Conde 1-0, and win at home, in their penultimate match against Paços de Ferreira by 3-1. In the week prior to the last match Mourinho was further surprised by news he was later able to confirm as being true.

"I was given two pieces of information that someone – whom I couldn't believe would do this – had forbidden an official supporters group to sing my name in the stands. As you know, there are official songs in the club for almost all of the club's players. Mine was vetoed. From that day on, I redoubled my efforts for the games to follow, while the information I had received proved to be true. No one ever sang my name again, with the exception of the Champions League final. There were many people at the game, members and supporters who didn't belong to any supporters group, and it was they who shouted and sang my name during the second half. Even so, I saw the official supporters club turn their backs while my name was being sung."

In the immediate future, all that was left was to prepare for the match against the Spanish team. Against Rio Ave, the starting line up had nothing to do with the players that would play in Coruña. José Mourinho had different training and preparation sessions.

Knowing Deportivo as well as he did, the Porto coach was very much aware of what to expect in Spain. He knew to expect 'hell' at the Riazor Stadium. A vibrant home crowd would be supporting their team from the very first to the last minute of the match – a crowd that was very confident following the draw they'd managed in the first tie. All of Galicia was caught up in a party atmosphere, as if they were already in the final. In addition to facing Deportivo, Porto would also have to 'take on' the Galician people.

The first obstacle came as they set off from the hotel, which was some 50 kilometres from the stadium. The police couldn't control the problems caused by heavy traffic and the bus only arrived at the Riazor an hour before kick-off, when UEFA rules state that teams should arrive one hour and forty-five minutes before the start. For José Mourinho *"The Porto bus was stuck in traffic on purpose, no doubt about it"*. Once the first obstacle was out of the way, another would have to be overcome on the pitch.

"Some ideas, without which we couldn't succeed, had been taken on board by the players. We had to control the game by holding on to the ball, never letting the opponent take the initiative, and never, never staking everything on counter-attacking. I knew we'd have to impress our opponents with a clearly mature approach. The first step in this direction came right at the start when we took control of the game. Usually, teams visiting the Riazor try to cope with the initial pressure for ten or twenty minutes. If they hold on without letting in a goal, then they develop their game. We didn't do that. As soon as the game began, we got hold of the ball, and didn't give them a chance to pressure us. I was always very direct with my players in telling them what I wanted. In the changing rooms, before the start of the game, I repeated to them that we only had two options: we either dominated or controlled the game. Never the other way round.

The Porto bus was stuck in traffic on purpose, no doubt about it

By dominating, I mean a team that attacks in the opponent's half, looking to score and having ball superiority. Controlling the game means playing further back, with all the spaces filled up, with a system designed to keep the ball, going on the attack with an objective, passing and circulating the ball

along the last line of men. I even admit to feigning injury in order to stop the game and reduce its intensity. I asked my players for domination and, only as a last resort, control."

That was probably the most important game of their lives and the FC Porto players were up to the task. Porto dominated the game from start to finish, and Derlei's goal in the second half meant a win for the Portuguese side to cap a fantastic display. The prize was a trip to Gelsenkirchen – unlike the match at the Stadium of the Dragon, those now celebrating were Portuguese.

At the end of the match, a very funny episode took place near the changing rooms. In the Riazor corridors, José Mourinho heard his name being called out. It was Luque, a Deportivo player who shouted, "*Mourinho, de puta madre*". Behind Mourinho stood Silvino Louro, who didn't like what he heard. He immediately ran up to Luque, all worked up: "*What do you want, you clown…you're the son of a b…*" Luque was astonished at what he heard, not understanding Silvino's attitude, who had to be calmed down. It was only when they reached the changing rooms that Silvino learnt that in Spanish "*de puta madre*" means "*fantastic*". Luque was only praising the Porto team and congratulating José Mourinho on his players' performance.

The next day, first thing in the morning, José Mourinho and his family were at Oporto's airport with tickets to London. Mourinho had told the journalists that if his family so wished, they could all go. He was to watch the other semi-final between Chelsea and Monaco, but Mourinho would only go with his family.

"The scout from my technical team, André Vilas Boas, always went. I wanted to go, but I also wanted to be with my family. Deep down I wanted to work, as well as unwind with my loved ones, nothing more. And why not? One thing didn't affect the other. During the day I would be with my wife and kids, and at night I'd go to the football. I know this didn't go down well with some people, but I really didn't care."

That's what he thought and that's what he did. José Mourinho spent the day with his family, went to the match, and a quarter of an hour later was back at the hotel with some of the journalists who had accompanied him. One of them had even been with him throughout the day. Stories of supposed meetings with agents were amongst the lies spread about that day.

The Stamford Bridge game decided whom FC Porto would face in the

Champions League final. It was to be the team José Mourinho had wished for since the start of the competition, only now it would be at the end: Monaco.

"There, we finally got Monaco and just as well it was to be in the final. With only one match, I knew the vast majority of fans at Gelsenkirchen would be on our side. Apart from there being more Porto fans, I also knew that they would be more 'fanatical' and more involved than the opponent's supporters – in contrast to Seville where the Celtic fans had 'dominated'. British players themselves are more emotional than the French, and so once again I preferred Monaco in the final. In addition, I was very sure that my team was better than that of Didier Deschamps'. So much so, that from the very beginning I was convinced I was going to be European champion."

Five days later, Porto played their last match of the Super League. It was 9 May and they beat Paços de Ferreira 3-1 at the Stadium of the Dragon.

> THE PORTUGUESE CUP FINAL

There were two finals left to play. The Portuguese Cup the following weekend, and the Champions League on 26 May. FC Porto, led by José Mourinho, would once again be involved in a national and an international cup final. Only now the timing would change. The Portuguese Cup would come first, followed by the Champions League final. It was with this calendar in mind that preparations began.

The group was aware that the game against Benfica had to be won. Mourinho asked his players not to think about the Monaco match, but this was impossible and the coach himself ended up being influenced by 'the match of their lives'.

"I knew that Monaco's coach would be observing us at the match and so I didn't put on what I considered to be my best team at the time. McCarthy played instead of Carlos Alberto and this change, in terms of strategy, altered everything. I sought to hide from Deschamps the way I would play in the final, and thus surprise him. As for my players, although I asked them not to think about anything else, I knew that would be impossible because the Champions League final would always be on their minds. In any event, I think we had a great game. After the first quarter of an hour and right up to the end, we dominated Benfica – even playing with only ten players as Jorge Costa was sent off in the second half. Perhaps the only thing that was missing was to 'get stuck in' with more determination, but that's the way it is when you have 'the match of your lives' coming up."

FC Porto's domination was not enough to win the Cup. Derlei scored a goal at the end of the first half and they were ahead for a while; but Benfica equalised in the second half. A goal by Simão Sabrosa, in extra-time, put paid to FC Porto's hopes of once again winning everything they could in the same season. The Portuguese Cup was lost, but once more José Mourinho used his psychology on his players.

"I told them that the Cup meant little compared with what was to come. For most people, winning the Champions League happens once in a lifetime. Winning the Portuguese Cup can happen many times.

In this way, I played down the defeat, asked them to forget the match

against Benfica, and said, 'I'll give you two days off to do whatever you like. Then we'll have a week to think about Monaco. Go home'."

This is what the FC Porto players did. Two days later they returned and from then on, just as Mourinho had said, no one thought of anything else except their opponents in the final. The obsession was called Monaco.

"In preparing for the game, we started by watching many of our opponent's games. I already knew everything about Monaco, but I wanted my players to know everything, too. Above all, I wanted them to see for themselves how fast Giuly was as he counter-attacked; how opportune Morientes, the goal-scorer was; how calm Rothen was as he led the team's attacks; as well as the whole way Monaco moved when attacking and defending. In addition to this general information, we did something we had never done before. Each player was given an individual DVD to look at and analyse. For example, I gave Paulo Ferreira a DVD on the collective and individual actions of Rothen, Monaco's winger who would be playing 'on top of' him. The central defenders had information on Morientes and Prso. Each player had his own DVD to study. Afterwards, we had a group discussion on the individual information gleaned. In this way, we got to know Monaco and I believe the French team held no secrets for us."

With all this knowledge of the opponent and with tactics adjusted accordingly, FC Porto left for Gelsenkirchen. A plane full of hope and hungry for glory landed in Germany on 24 May.

> THE CHAMPIONS LEAGUE FINAL

(This section is written by José Mourinho)

I looked at the electric cube hanging over the pitch. 80 minutes, 3-0. I analysed the game and sensed the confidence, tranquillity, cohesion and joy of the team. I turned around to André and Rui Faria and said, *"That's it, we're European Champions!"* Then I looked back at the bench, and smiled at the other assistants, who were waving at me and giving me the thumbs up. It was done. I started to think about a lot of things, something I had never done at a football match before: the road taken, a childhood full of dreams, obstacles, critics, criticism, family, beliefs, untiring fans, history, immortality, the threats I'd received the day before.

I had been at a training session and, as always, the only link to the outside world was the private mobile phone that only my wife knows about. I had also blocked all outside calls to the hotel. I thought about the game, prepared myself for it mentally, thought about the players and tried to tap into their psychological state of mind. I surrounded myself with my assistants and we developed our collective spirit and sense of worth.

At around 10:30 pm, I went up to my room, to enjoy my brand new Sony Vaio and unwind with *The Punisher*, starring John Travolta. Unexpectedly, someone knocked at the door. I opened it and there was one of the Club's directors, Reinaldo Teles. "*Sorry, but I have eight urgent messages on my mobile phone for you."* They were from someone who had identified himself and therefore deserved a return call, I thought. On the other end of the line, there quickly came a death threat linked to my arrival back in Oporto.

"You think you're the best... you bastard... we won't do anything now because you have a final to play tomorrow, but as soon as its over, consider yourself a dead man, because we'll get you, and as soon as you get back to Oporto your fate is sealed. You don't have a chance..."

Incredulous, I replied, *"You must be mad... I don't know what you're talking about or why you're saying these things, but I think you must be mad..."*

I immediately hung up. Reinaldo Teles, who'd understood the content of the conversation, was dumbstruck, but quickly told me not to worry. He assured me everything would be sorted out. We went down together to the hotel lobby and I told my assistants what was happening. I saw the look of astonishment on their faces, as well as some concern, as the 'character', who had made the call, was well-known in Oporto's underworld and had a criminal record – several convictions and suspended sentences. According to the police, who had by then been contacted, he had to be taken seriously and surveillance was to be stepped up, especially as he led an organised group, which made it more difficult for the police to control the situation. The fact that a crowd was expected at the airport and in the city of Oporto merely made matters worse.

The following day, Pinto da Costa came to me and assured me of my safety. He said not to worry about my family's or my own security as this would be guaranteed.

Curiously, this was the only match where Porto didn't take its own private security along.

When Kim Nielsen blew the final whistle, all I could think of were my wife and kids. They were in the stands and would be travelling on another plane. Security had been set up for them, but on their own initiative some of the Club's employees, aware of the threat and the protection they were under, brought them from the stands to the pitch. There was relief, joy and emotion – unforgettable emotions. The four of us shared a hug, kisses, smiles and tears, while Zé – bewildered by it all – asked why we were crying if we had won the final.

I wanted to leave immediately, but Matilde said no way. She said the Cup was mine, the medal was mine, and I had to make the most of it – I had to touch the star that had shone down on me once again. I went over to the pitch and proudly took in the happiness of a fantastic group that climbed up on to the podium of European football history.

Before going onto the pitch, I had told them, *"We'll never forget this day; the emotions, the sensations, the images will stay with us for the rest of our lives. Living with bad memories is a tragedy; living with good ones gives us the strength to carry on fighting. Be yourselves, don't lose your identity as a team, play like hell, and win!"*

With each passing minute we saw less of Mónaco and more of Porto

For the first time, I waited for them at the door to the changing rooms and kissed them all. 26 May 2004, Gelsenkirchen: We were immortal.

My family was close by and I didn't want to lose them again. I wanted them in my line of vision at the post-match interviews, next to me at the press conference and, with the precious help of the Club's employees, also on our plane. With me forever.

We arrived in Oporto. On the one side there were the celebrations, and on the other the security operation organised by me and some friends, in the silence of the previous night – the night when I should have been resting and relaxing in preparation for the game. Everything was perfect. There were two buses on the runway that took us home and let me see the celebrations on television – my party, the party I had contributed towards but could not join. My work at FC Porto was complete. I didn't leave as I had wished; I left in the way someone else wanted me to. A way which was easier for those who don't like to lose.

My life had changed. Professionally, I went from Leiria to the top of the world in only three years; and socially, the change was no less significant: the end of privacy, invasion of privacy, disrespect for the principles my family and I defend, lies, slander, persecution, the need for private security 24 hours a day…I could now understand the behaviour of world famous figures that is sometimes criticised. As a great friend of mine said, *"It's a tough life, a very tough life"*.

But let's return to Gelsenkirchen and the match. We were really well prepared. The eight days of training gave us the peace of mind to cover all the variables of the game. We knew Monaco like the back of our hands; we knew what to do with our eyes closed at each moment and in every situation. We were confident because we had an answer for everything.

We started off looking to control the game, lines a bit further back, safety at the back, a well-developed collective sense. The players clearly understood that if we didn't dominate, then at least we should control the game. I really felt that, we had to control, drop back a bit, slow Giuly down, take some freedom away from Deco in order to cut off their attacks, and control emotions. Perfect. With each passing minute we saw less of Monaco and more of Porto; more security, more control. Danger was lurking around their goal.

Giuly's injury meant the opposition had to make some changes, and so did we. Less speed and more danger in the final third. This implied greater pressure from us, greater safety and less concern about creating spaces at the back of our defensive line, where Paulo Ferreira had kept Monaco's best player out of the game. This had happened with Giggs, Luque and now Rothen. Baía was really strong, Jorge Costa ferocious, Ricardo Carvalho imperious in controlling Morientes, and Nuno Valente solid as ever.

I thought we'd make it to half-time all square, but then Carlos Alberto scored.

I started to prepare my speech for half-time. The tactical approach to changes in the game, the certainty that we'd have more space to attack, as well as the changes that would be brought about by Nonda going on. Also, the need for discernment in terms of our passing and to be objective in what we were doing. From a mental point of view, to be on our guard for the opponent's attempt to react by taking control of the game, the urgent need for greater involvement from players like Costinha, Deco or Derlei, who had yet to show what they were capable of, and indifference to the next goal, be it 1-1 or 2-0.

The game was under control, but I thought we could finish it off. My number 10 needed freedom to play. He had to get away from the pressure of Zikos and Cissé in order to go down the flanks more and between the lines. Alenitchev moved into the number 10 position, thus freeing up Deco.

Zikos hesitated between chasing Deco out of the central axis and staying put in his position, thus giving Deco more room to move. This confusion on their part led to our second goal. *Finito*, in the words of Dimitri Alenitchev,

who ended up finishing off the game and taking us to the gates of Olympus. I looked at Tami and the kids in front of me and felt what I described earlier. At the same time I felt the sweaty arm of my captain around me; he'd risked a yellow card by leaving the field to give me a hug, and said, *"You're the best, we're champions!"* This was better than getting the medal I would now add to the UEFA Cup, and the European Super Cup and the Cup Winners Cup won with Barcelona, making me the only Portuguese ever to win all three UEFA competitions. As usual, no one has yet remembered this.

I wanted to keep up the fast pace and brought on Benny, all loose, happy and mobile

I wanted to keep up the fast pace and brought on Benny, all loose, happy and mobile. He was able to keep the ball far away from our defence, and to put pressure on the opponent's back line and keep them there. Later on I decided to put on Pedro Emanuel, a champion. Ready to fight all year round, he was efficient and solid. If anyone deserved to play, it was him, the third midfielder. Then we were into the closing stages: total control, the opponent's disbelief, and the end of the game.

The Cup was beautiful. I had been courting it the day before, but hadn't dared touch it. I saw my reflection in it, I breathed it in and stood at its side – but I didn't touch it. Now I got up on stage and received the medal from Len Johanssen, who said, *"See you in August at the Monaco gala"*. I went up to the Cup and kissed it.

After the party started, so did my escape to safety – or so I thought at the time, without knowing what was to come in the days that followed.

First of all, I was subjected to a campaign of rumour and slander. Then I was hounded and had people waiting at the entrance to my home, threatening both my loved ones and me. For the first time in my life, I was forced to hire private security. They were dramatic and unforgettable weeks of terror.

> THE MOVE TO CHELSEA

(This section is written by José Mourinho)

Who is telling the truth?

In the world of football news travels fast. Journalists carry out their research, there are sources within the clubs, directors contact each other, and agents try to anticipate situations. Everything involves business, commissions and transfers – the quest for a much sought-after 'trophy' – taking on Fellini-like proportions.

It was said that, among the most important clubs, Liverpool, Chelsea and Inter were interested in me. Suddenly, eight different agents – Portuguese, Brazilian, Italian, Spanish, English and Dutch, besieged me. All of them were 'friends' of Abramovich or Peter Kenyon, of Rick Parry or Massimo Moratti. They all had meetings set up, and wanted to be involved in my possible transfer to one of these clubs.

I started to be inundated with calls at home; people exercised their influence; and many promises were made. Sometimes, the pressure reached levels worthy of a Don Corleone.

A meeting had been set up with Liverpool, in Manchester, for the eve of the Champions League final, but I declined. Another meeting with Moratti in Nice had been cancelled, as had the wish to work in yet another highly motivated and challenging country. Let's not be hypocritical, financial matters were also important. As my dear Rivaldo had said when he wanted to get a better contract with Barcelona, *"When I went to the solicitor to sign the property deeds, they didn't accept medals, not even the FIFA Golden Ball award."*

I wanted to experience Porto forever – our career, ambitions and motivation. And so, I isolated myself. I said that I didn't want to go to any meetings or make any decisions. I expressed these wishes publicly. Also that any club or agent involved in this process had to wait until the end of the season to make any big decisions – and they had to contact Mr Pinto da Costa beforehand.

The weeks flew by. FC Porto were also flying. We were national champions, and we'd made it to the semi-finals of the Champions League. Chelsea stepped up the pace and dismissed Ranieri, making the front pages in the English press. The research began, and the agents attacked in force.

One day an Italian came to my house, along with a Portuguese man. They said they were close friends of Abramovich and that they'd sort the situation out. Then a Dutchman sent me a document stating he was an agent for some of the Chelsea players and, as such, had been mandated to deal with the matter. In turn, a Spaniard was to take care of Ronaldinho's transfer from Barcelona to Chelsea, and was therefore hand in glove with Chelsea. And a Brazilian phoned to say that he was in Paris, in a meeting with another Portuguese and Abramovich, in order to move the transfer process along. After hanging up the call from Paris, the telephone rang again. Jorge Mendes was with Abramovich (plus Peter Kenyon and Eugene Tanenbaum) on his private plane, in Vigo, and wanted to speak to me.

Truth be told, I thought very fast. Jorge had won the right to take charge of negotiations by being honest. Also, FC Porto, the Club's President and the Board trusted him. Thus, there wouldn't be any secrets and I could publicly express my wish to move abroad, in search of new emotions, challenges and experiences – and, who knows, great difficulties that would force me to make further progress and become an even better coach. I didn't want to be the best coach at 40 and a has-been at 50.

The talks with Abramovich were formal and I gave my word that I would not sign with another club without giving Chelsea the first opportunity to do so. I merely said that matters relating to my contract with FC Porto had to be settled satisfactorily with the Club, and that Jorge Mendes and his assistant would be responsible for my contract and its clauses. Also, my acceptance would be based on a discussion, to take place after the end of the season, related to the definition of objectives, the structural conditions to carry them through, the building of the squad, and the definition of leadership and methodology.

FC Porto were informed of my wish to leave and knew that Jorge Mendes would be responsible for all negotiations. They were also aware of my interest in certain players, and – above all – they knew that being competitive by nature, nothing would distract me from my work. Criticism started to pour in from certain quarters in Portuguese football. To all this I replied with a win in Coruña, and qualification for the Champions League final.

The period that followed was sad, very sad. People who were frustrated by their inability to win the race, launched on a path hitherto completely unknown to me: that of hatred, slander, threats and vengeance. But let's talk of good things!

On the Friday after Gelsenkirchen, I travelled to Nice with Jorge Mendes and his financial adviser, Luis Correia. We took a helicopter to Monaco, and then a speed boat to the monumental *Pelorus*, Roman Abramovich's private yacht. There, my future boss was waiting for me, together with Peter Kenyon and Eugene Tanenbaum. Some weeks before, I had told them that we would speak in person at a later stage, without worrying about the competition from other big clubs.

It was a fantastic welcome: the grand yacht; the elegance; the straightforwardness of the three men; their congratulating me on the European title; the delicious meal; the beauty of the scenery; and the start of a new life with the Lions of West London.

We spent a few days on the yacht, with the full knowledge of FC Porto and its President. We spoke a great deal, discussed many ideas, came to certain conclusions, and signed a four-year contract.

In this way, José Mourinho brought to a close his career in Portugal – his cycle of victories; a Super Cup, the Portuguese Cup, two National Championships, the UEFA Cup and the Champions League.

It was a brilliant time. For José Mourinho – now a respected coach with a truly impressive set of trophies, given his short career as a head coach. For his players – now more well-rounded professionals than ever before, more respected abroad, and with more medals. And also for FC Porto, as it enriched its trophy room – now the largest in Portugal when it comes to UEFA competitions. Porto is also wealthier in terms of its bank balance.

Whether or not you like José Mourinho, it doesn't take much to understand his significance in the history of the club.